FURTHER *along* THE WAY

**NATIONAL LIBRARY OF AUSTRALIA CATALOGUING-
IN-PUBLICATION ENTRY : (PAPERBACK)**

Creator: Manley, Ken R., author.

Title: Further along the way / Ken Manley.

ISBN: 9780994572554 (paperback)

ISBN: 9780994572561 (ebook)

Subjects: Bible. John--Criticism, interpretation, etc. Christianity.

FURTHER *along* THE WAY

MORE PERSONAL ENCOUNTERS WITH JESUS IN JOHN'S GOSPEL

KEN R MANLEY

Morling Press
First Published 2017
122 Herring Rd Macquarie Park NSW 2113 Australia
Phone: +61 2 9878 0201
Email: enquiries@morling.edu.au
www.morlingcollege.com

© Morling Press 2017

This publication is copyright. Other than for the purposes of study and subject to the conditions of the Copyright Act, no part of it in any form or by any means (electronic, mechanical, micro-copying, photocopying or otherwise) may be reproduced, stored in a retrieval system or transmitted without the permission of the publisher.

The Scripture quotations contained herein are from the New Revised Standard Version Bible, copyright, 1989, by the Division of Christian Education of the National Council of the Churches of Christ in the U.S.A. Used by permission. All rights reserved.

ISBN: 978-0-9945725-5-4 (paperback)
ISBN: 978-0-9945725-6-1 (e-book)

Designed by Brugel Images & Design www.brugel.com.au

CONTENTS

COMMENDATIONS   IX

PREFACE   XIII

INTRODUCTION   1

Chapter One
**A VOICE IN THE DESERT:
JESUS AND JOHN THE BAPTIST**   5
(John 1:19–37)
Questions for discussion...15

CHAPTER TWO
**IN MY FATHER'S HOUSE:
JESUS AND THE LOAN SHARKS**   17
(John 2:13–25)
Questions for discussion...27

CHAPTER THREE
**LONG-DISTANCE FAITH:
JESUS AND A WORRIED FATHER**   29
(John 4:43–54)
Questions for discussion...37

CHAPTER FOUR
**DO YOU WANT TO BE MADE WELL?
JESUS AND THE DISABLED MAN** *39*

(John 5:1–18)
Questions for discussion. 49

CHAPTER FIVE
**IMAGINE ALL THE PEOPLE:
JESUS AND THE HUNGRY CROWD** *51*

(John 6:1–15)
Questions for discussion. 60

CHAPTER SIX
**COME OUT IN THE OPEN:
JESUS AND HIS BROTHERS** *63*

(John 7:1–13)
Questions for discussion. 73

CHAPTER SEVEN
**KNOWING WHO I AM:
JESUS AND 'THE JEWS'** *75*

(John 8:12–59)
Questions for discussion. 84

CHAPTER EIGHT
**THE CROOKED TREASURER:
JESUS AND JUDAS** *87*

(John 13:21–30)
Questions for discussion. 96

CHAPTER NINE
**THOSE WHO WILL BELIEVE IN ME:
JESUS AND THE BELIEVERS OF ALL AGES** *99*

(John 17:1–26)
Questions for discussion. 109

CHAPTER TEN
**HERE IS YOUR MOTHER:
JESUS AND MARY** *111*

(John 19:25–27)
Questions for discussion. 118

CHAPTER ELEVEN
**I HAVE SEEN THE LORD:
JESUS AND MARY MAGDALENE** *121*

(John 20:1–18)

Questions for discussion. 133

CHAPTER TWELVE
**WHAT IS GOING TO HAPPEN TO HIM?
JESUS AND THE DISCIPLE WHOM HE LOVED** *135*

(John 21:1–25)

Questions for discussion. 145

CONCLUSION *147*

READING GUIDE *153*

COMMENDATIONS

'In contemporary western society there is a continuing fascination with the person of Jesus despite the fact that people are increasingly disinterested in organised religion. Ken Manley's *Further Along the Way* well illustrates why this interest in Jesus continues. This sequel to his earlier book *On the Way to Faith* continues to explore Jesus' encounters with people as recorded in John's Gospel. Ken Manley's thoughtful insights provide stimulating challenges for readers with a desire to explore Jesus and his interaction with people in a variety of contexts.

'*Further Along the Way* is an excellent resource for home group Bible studies associated with a preaching/teaching series from John's Gospel. With helpful questions associated with each encounter, the book is a welcome resource for individuals, groups and preachers. I warmly commend this book to individuals and groups wanting to explore the challenge of a personal encounter with Jesus.'

REV KEITH JOBBERNS, *NATIONAL MINISTRIES DIRECTOR, AUSTRALIAN BAPTIST MINISTRIES*

'After the feast of insights from Rev Dr Ken Manley's first book of reflections on John's Gospel, *On the Way to Faith,* I was delighted to find there were twelve baskets (or chapters) left over! So here we are invited to explore *Further Along the Way*, as we examine more encounters of Jesus with a wide range of people in the Fourth Gospel.

'Again, Ken is the ideal reading companion for such a journey of faith—closely attending to the text of John, with a judicious use of excellent scholarship, some moving personal experiences, contemporary film, poetry and music, and all woven together with warmth and wit, comfort and challenge, profound trust and truth.

'But be warned! If you're looking for a comfortable, non-challenging travelling companion who quotes pious platitudes at every opportunity and avoids the hard questions of life, faith and the Bible, this book will demand much more of you. Ken does not shy away from difficult questions about John's distinctive narrative and emphases—about variations in the ancient manuscripts of John (where relevant), or the attitude to "the Jews" or the family of Jesus, or the convoluted Church traditions about Mary (both of them). Rather, such issues are discussed with honesty and sensitivity, taking account of the wider literary and cultural contexts, then and now, and we are guided helpfully through them to the central themes of John's account of the Word become flesh.

'This book will be a wonderful resource for Bible studies (questions are provided at the end of each chapter), for personal study and for sermon preparation (further references are also provided)—and just simply for reading and reflecting on the revelation of God through Jesus as recounted in the most distinctive of the four Gospels.'

DR KEITH DYER, ASSOC PROF OF NEW TESTAMENT, WHITLEY COLLEGE, UNIVERSITY OF DIVINITY, MELBOURNE

'In 2014 the good people of Canterbury Baptist Church and I gave the whole of term one to studying Ken's earlier text *On The Way to Faith*. This fed our sermon series and our small groups. It nurtured our leadership and reached our fringes. This has remained a foundation in this congregation's life of discipleship, community, and mission.

'The call prevails and the journey continues. I have no hesitation in recommending this sequel for that task. We still need to be encountering this Christ in today's settings. We still need to be 'on the way' whether we are moving through familiar or fraught places. This is a journey my congregation and I will gladly take up afresh through this sequel. I am delighted to be heading *Further Along the Way* again with Christ's company and Ken Manley's inspiration.'

REV. GORDON WILD, SENIOR PASTOR, CANTERBURY BAPTIST CHURCH, VICTORIA

Commendations

'Informed by serious scholarship, but infused with a deep personal faith, Ken Manley's reflections on encounters with Jesus invite us to re-encounter Jesus ourselves. He has managed that rare combination of being readable yet thoughtful, making these reflections ideal for personal devotion or group study. I love the Australian flavour he brings, helping us to meet Jesus under our southern sky.'

REV MEGAN POWELL DU TOIT, *AUSTRALIAN COLLEGE OF THEOLOGY, SYDNEY*

'Ken Manley offers warmly inviting and deeply engaging readings of familiar yet sometimes difficult episodes from the Gospel of John. He brings us face to face with Jesus encountering people at different stages of faith in surprising and grace-filled ways. He explores how what really is good news about Jesus engages with the concerns of our world and generation. *Further Along the Way* is an inspiring and accessible resource for preachers, small groups, or any curious reader wanting to freshly explore John and open to meeting Jesus in new and fresh ways. I am looking forward to using it to invite our church to recalibrate our lives as disciples around these surprising and countercultural encounters of Jesus.'

REV DR DARREN CRONSHAW, *PASTOR OF AUBURNLIFE, MISSION CATALYST WITH BAPTIST UNION OF VICTORIA*

'Ken Manley's book *On the Way to Faith* was recently used by our whole church in both small groups and Sunday services to spiritually nourish us as we encountered Jesus in John's Gospel. Ken has a wonderful way of bringing robust and erudite scholarship to bear on these studies, but also deftly weaves the pastoral and everyday realities of life into them so as to make them engaging and helpful. Having read Ken's follow up book, *Further Along the Way*, I am certain that churches with a passion for both good theology and a healthy Christian spirituality will be greatly assisted by it.'

REV NICHOLAS TUOHY, *SENIOR PASTOR, KEW BAPTIST CHURCH, VICTORIA*

'Ken Manley once again reminds us that the gospel of John is a text for our time. As he engages with the encounters Jesus had with communities and groups, as well as individuals, our contemporary obsession with personal spirituality is not so much critiqued as it is gently expanded. We encounter the Jesus whose hopes for humanity extended beyond personal salvation to address the profound spiritual hunger of the whole world which God so loved. The faith we discover is both miraculous and grounded, taught and demonstrated, lived out and believed in.'

REV CAROLYN FRANCIS, *COLLINS ST BAPTIST CHURCH, MELBOURNE*

PREFACE

This book is a sequel to *On the Way to Faith* (2013) in which I discussed twelve individual personal encounters with Jesus as recorded in John's Gospel.[1] Some sequels are unnecessary and of limited value—they may disappoint those who enjoyed the original. However, sequels can be valuable and the sequel has an ancient literary heritage. Homer's *Odyssey* is regarded as a sequel to the *Iliad*—not that any such ambitions or parallels are relevant in this case! This book is offered as a continuation and expansion of what some readers have found to be helpful— an invitation to travel along the road to faith.

I have prepared this second book simply because there are many more encounters with Jesus told in John—stories which also encourage us into a personal meeting with the Jesus whom John affirms to be the Son of God. Although we live in a vastly different and distant age, we are invited into a similar experience of discovery and discipleship.

One difference from *On the Way to Faith* is that some of these studies refer to groups rather than individuals: the moneychangers in the temple (John 2:13–25), the crowd fed with loaves and fishes (John 6:1–15), his brothers (John 7:1–13), the 'Jews' (John 8:12–30) and believers across all ages (John 17:1–26). Yet in each case the encounter with Jesus was decisive and instructive.

I have retained the 'sermon' format since that again is the origin of most of these studies, although each one has been carefully revised. To move from an aural experience to the written word can sometimes be problematic. I am encouraged, however, by Sally Warhaft's observation that 'speeches repay quiet contemplation as much as eager listening. Imagination and curiosity can conquer the lapse of time'.[2]

I hope that these studies will provoke the imagination and curiosity of readers as they explore John's gospel in their personal study and in home groups.

Among the letters I received after the first volume was a short note of thanks from a senior lady who commented that reading it was 'a bit like a cow let into a new paddock who quickly devoured the fresh, juicy, sweet grass and then retired to ruminate. I related so strongly to much in it with tears of joy at finding such treasures'. This humbling response has been part of the motivation for this volume, which I hope will encourage further 'rumination' by many others.

Once again, I am indebted to Morling Press for their enthusiastic agreement to undertake this venture. Sheree Brugel has again been most helpful at every point of preparation. My friend Barbara Coe has, once again, placed me in her debt by her careful editing of the first draft. Peter Friend of Morling has also greatly helped with his professional editing skills in the final draft.

Most of all I am grateful to my wife, Margaret, who continues to encourage me but has also endured many hours downstairs as I have retreated upstairs to my study—although I am assured that not having me 'under her feet' in retirement years has proved to be a significant blessing. One of the grandchildren told me a while back that when she was quite young she thought I lived in the study, but now as an adult she knows it to be true.

My prayer is that my grandchildren will understand better what I have been doing and—more significantly—many others will be encouraged to explore the way to faith that John's gospel invites us to discover.

Ken R Manley

---

1   K R Manley, *On the Way to Faith: Personal Encounters with Jesus in John's Gospel* (Macquarie Park: Morling Press, 2013). The passages discussed in this book are: 1:35–51; 2:1–12; 2:23–3:20; 4:3–42; 7:53–8:1; 9:1–41; 11:1–46; 12:1–8; 13:1–20; 18:28–40; 20:19–30; 21:1–19.

2   S Warhaft (ed), *Well May We Say ... The Speeches that Made Australia* (Melbourne: Black, 2004), p. xii.

INTRODUCTION

Authentic religious experience remains a central quest of humanity. Innumerable examples of this in our modern world may be found—the bewildering range of 'new' religions as well as the revival of many ancient religions. For those seriously wishing to explore and experience the inner meaning and power of Christianity, the Gospel of John remains a key resource.

The image of religious experience as being on a journey of discovery has a long history and remains vital for contemporary seekers. Linked with this idea of being 'on the way' is the notion of a transforming encounter with the Divine. This has been an important way of reading the gospels and many have found the reality of Christ through the sensitive reading of stories about individuals or even groups who encountered Jesus Christ. If you are genuinely hoping to learn more about Jesus and what it means to be a believer then the Gospel of John is an excellent place to start.

An influential book among an earlier generation of students was JH Oldham's *Life is Commitment* (1953). He helped many readers face their difficulties in believing but also asserted:

> Those who have encountered Christ and made a wholehearted response to that encounter have found an answer to the problem of man and truth. They have been

> given a faith which they do not have to carry, but which carries them. It is the testimony of Christians that amid all the uncertainties of relativism they have discovered that to which they may surrender themselves in complete trust ... What they have known and experienced of love is something that they believe will hold firm in all the stress and tests of life and prove stronger than death itself.[1]

These are themes which any reader of John will hear. There are of course real problems in jumping from the New Testament era into our 21st century. However, around the world today millions of people are still fascinated by Jesus of Nazareth and discover in his character and teaching answers to fundamental questions about life and its purpose. This invitation to pilgrimage comes from an ancient document that is still remarkably relevant and challenging.

As we study John today we are able to utilise some of the devout and exacting scholarship that has explored every possible nuance of interpretation across the centuries. We can also be confident that we have an accurate text and can explore for ourselves this foundational document of the Christian religion.

Even the most cursory reader of the four gospels knows that the Fourth Gospel has a somewhat different character from the other three. John is sometimes called 'a spiritual gospel', which is precisely the description given to it by Clement of Alexandria (150–215 CE), one of the important early Church Fathers. Significantly, Clement also claimed that John was 'inspired by the Spirit' (see 2 Timothy 3:16). Of course the other gospels are also decidedly 'spiritual' in what they teach. However, in John we find powerful symbols and metaphors often integrated into stories of personal encounters.

The mysticism in John—an awareness of the divine presence in the stories—speaks suggestively to a modern reader. Moving seamlessly from an encounter story to profound teaching by Jesus is a repeated pattern and the reader is simply carried along from narrative to discourse. John creatively weaves together events with profound theological insights.

That is why we will need an open mind and spiritual imagination if these stories are to teach us. They contain early witnesses to the powerful challenge that

Jesus presented to real people, as diverse as a seemingly weird prophet, greedy moneychangers, a man sick with worry about his dying child, and many others. One man began as a disciple, was invited into the inner group of followers, and saw and heard Jesus in the most intimate of ways. Sadly, his later denial and treachery led to his name becoming a byword for apostasy. All these encounters retain meaning and relevance for us today. Only as we admit our deepest needs and welcome the possibilities of transformation can we hope to discover something of ourselves in these stories and be brought closer to an authentic faith in Jesus.

Once again, the hope is that as we reflect on stories of how Jesus challenged and inspired these people we too may encounter the living Jesus and move further along the way to faith. Remember that the author specifically tells us that these stories have a theological and religious intent—they were written 'so that you might believe that Jesus is the Messiah, the Son of God, and that through believing you may have life in his name' (John 20:31). His aim is 'not simply to inform but, more significantly, to transform'.[2]

In John we are introduced to what the theologian von Balthasar has called 'a progressive entrance of the believing person into the total reality of faith'.[3] He elaborated the meaning of experience through the same 'journey' metaphor that has been adopted in these two studies with an invitation to find more of this 'total reality of faith'.

This is an invitation to meet Christ, not to embark on complex theological disputes or debate denominational differences. As Oldham asserted: 'I am confident that if a single ray of light reaches a man from Christ, penetrates into his being and influences his way of living, he is further along the road of true belief in Him than if he gave his unreflecting assent to a multitude of orthodox propositions which have no perceptible effect upon his conduct'.[4]

These studies are designed to help us move 'further along the road of true belief'. And what is 'true belief' or faith? To discover the answer will challenge us to open our minds and venture into new places, as Lesslie Newbigin explained:

All the evidence of human experience, the evidence of the greatest of the poets, the artists, the scientists and the saints, goes to suggest that knowledge is accessible to those who are ready to keep the door open, to venture beyond what is clear and unquestionable, even if it involves the risk of being mistaken or talking nonsense ... the active principle is the willingness to go beyond what is certain, to listen beyond what is certain, to listen to what is not yet clear, to search for what is hardly visible, to venture the affirmation which may prove to be wrong, but which may also prove to be the starting point for new conquests of the mind. In the traditional language of Christianity the name for that active principle is faith.[5]

1 JH Oldham, *Life is Commitment* (London: SCM, 1953), p. 130.

2 D Lee, *Hallowed in Truth and Love. Spirituality in the Johannine Literature* (Preston, Vic: Mosaic, 2011), p. 14.

3 H Urs von Balthasar, as quoted by AJ Kelly and FJ Moloney, *Experiencing God in the Gospel of John* (New York: Paulist Press, 2003), pp. 7–8.

4 Oldham, *Life is Commitment*, p. 130.

5 L Newbigin, *Honest Religion for Secular Man* (London: Westminster, 1966), p. 93.

'Isenheim Altarpiece', Matthias Grünewald, 1512–1516

CHAPTER ONE

A VOICE IN THE DESERT: JESUS AND JOHN THE BAPTIST
(JOHN 1:19–37)

Preparation is everything. This is how we advise students anticipating an examination or an applicant hoping for a job. Yes, spontaneity is also welcomed, but in almost every human activity preparation remains crucial. The coming of God into our midst—the story of this gospel—needed a special preparation that stretched across long ages.

So as we begin to read John's gospel, seeking to trace encounters between Jesus and his contemporaries, our first such encounter is markedly different from those which follow. This one is all about preparations and beginnings. When John the Baptist greeted Jesus down near the River Jordan, religious and social change was in the air. Many hoped that the long-promised deliverance of God's chosen people—all humanity in fact—was imminent.

JOHN THE BAPTIST AS THE GREAT PREPARER

This story about how John met Jesus immediately plunges us into questions about beginnings and identity. Asking who John is leads us into a discovery about who Jesus is. John is the great preparer and that is why our gospel begins with his arrival on the stage of history.

Well, it almost begins with John. To understand who John is, and what his role is in the great story of Jesus, the gospel pushes even further back: before creation and time. The gospel opens with a breathtaking vision of who Jesus is (John 1:1–18). Beginning with an echo of Genesis 1—'in the beginning'—John points to the eternal origins of Jesus: 'In the beginning was the Word, and the Word was with God, and the Word was God' (1:1). This Word—which, we soon learn, is how the writer invites us to think about Jesus Christ—is the source of 'all things'; and the 'life' in him is 'the light of all people'.

John the Baptist is introduced in this majestic poem about the Word (1:6–8, 15). When we are told that he was 'sent from God' a theme of the gospel is introduced—this is a story about 'sentness'. God sent John in order to prepare for the coming of Jesus who repeatedly claimed that he had been sent from God. Even more, this same Jesus sends his followers. So John was the first one sent but he was the first in a long line of sent ones, or—to use another favourite word of the gospel—of witnesses.

John the Baptist links that Eternal Word and the messy reality of our world. The story of the Eternal Word becoming flesh (1:18) is the main event of all human history, and the somewhat bizarre figure of John is prominent in that salvation-event as the great preparer.

Another detail about John is immediately inserted into the long poem about the Word. He was 'a witness to testify to the light' (1:7). Lest there be any confusion, the writer informs us that John was most certainly not the light but only a witness to the light: 'The true light which enlightens everyone was coming into the world' (1:9).

That is solid theology and makes breathtaking claims about the Word. Remember this is the man Jesus Christ—who was 'coming into the world'. He was the true or real light but John had a role to play. He pointed to Jesus who would eventually specifically make his claim: 'I am the light of the world' (8:12).

Most of us have had opportunity to visit some beautiful caves. I vividly recall the first time I went to the Jenolan Caves, west of Sydney in the famous Blue Mountains. Actually, there are nine spectacular caves, with pure underground rivers and astonishing limestone formations. In most commercially developed caves there is a common practice: the tour stops and the lights are turned out. This is blackness that we never see above ground. Without light our eyes will never be able to see in that place. When the lights are turned back on we gradually adjust our eyes and are relieved that with the light now shining in the darkness we can continue to explore the caves.

That reminds us of the thrilling claim of Jesus. Throughout this gospel is a recurring theme. The 'world' is in darkness and Jesus is the transforming light, although the gospel will repeatedly insist: 'the light has come into the world but people loved darkness rather than light because their deeds were evil' (3:19).

John was someone who prepared people to 'see the light' that was Jesus. How does one 'testify to the light'? John gives us an idea. He warned people about the consequences of living in the dark underground caves of life. People were alerted and alarmed about his dramatic assertion that they faced imminent judgement and should turn away from sin and return to God. This was John's preparation, and then, when he could, he pointed straight to Jesus. That is how he testified to the light. That is how he prepared people to hear the message of Jesus. As John (and prophets of every age) discovered, however, not everyone welcomes the straight word and the demand for change.

JOHN THE BAPTIST PREPARED THE WAY OUT IN THE DESERT

The verse from Isaiah 40 cited in 1:23 was originally a word of comfort and hope to Jewish exiles in Babylon. 'I am the voice of one crying out in the wilderness, "Make straight the way of the Lord".' This is how John is identified in all four gospels (Matthew 3:3, Mark 1:3, Luke 3:4–6). The verse may mean the voice is located in the wilderness or that we are to make the way straight out in the desert. On either understanding the message is clear: make the way straight for the coming of the Lord. Just as engineers take care to clear away obstacles and construct a straight highway, so people are challenged to sweep away all life's rubbish and put their lives in order. Preparation is essential.

The relationship between John the Baptist and Jesus is a fascinating theme. As he is depicted in the other gospels, John is a somewhat scary character. 'John was prophetic even in utero,' suggests Bill Leonard[1]—he kicked for joy in his mother's womb as she greeted the embryonic presence of Jesus in Mary (Luke 1:44). Born into an aged priestly family, John came of age in the desert of Judea, possibly linked with the remote Jewish community at Qumran.

Deserts have shaped many a prophet. Some seem only able to sense the presence of God when away from human contact; the deafening silence makes one listen carefully for what Thomas Kelly called 'the holy whisper'.[2] Those years out in the desert certainly made John the man he became. Herman Hesse described another prophet, and we can easily use this to think about John the Baptist:

> For many years the sun seared and parched him. He scraped his knees on rock and sand as he prayed. He waited, fasting, for the sun to set before he chewed his few dates. Devils tormented him with temptation, mockery and trials, but he struck them down with prayer, with penitence, with renunciation of self ...[3]

John appeared from the desert with blazing eyes and a message that both alarmed and excited hearers. Travellers were transfixed as John shouted a message of fiery condemnation. Crowds of Jews—even tax collectors and soldiers—were shocked into repentance and were baptised in the Jordan confessing their sins. This was a pledge to begin a new way of life in preparation for the long-promised Messiah who was about to come.

This was a religious revival movement amongst Judean Jews. Whenever a religious revival erupts various responses usually follow. Some outsiders are critical of the whole phenomenon as superstition, and others, from within the faith, nibble away with doctrinal doubts about the revivalist. When Billy Graham came to Australia in 1959, I was a young student pastor in Sydney. I recall how the intellectuals and the media scoffed, whilst some liberals, as well as some narrow traditionalists, were critical of his methods and his theology. Only when the Crusade meetings were successful—Australia came close to a religious revival—did these critics mute their attacks.

Something like this happened when John began to attract huge numbers out there at the River Jordan; he had such an impact that he alarmed Jewish leaders concerned about religious orthodoxy and Roman officials anxious about law and order. But John the Baptist played a unique role as a witness. He became 'the normative image of the Christian preacher, apostle and missionary, the perfect prototype of the true evangelist, whose one goal is self-effacement before Christ'.[4]

JOHN THE BAPTIST WAS SURE OF HIS IDENTITY AND HIS UNIQUE ROLE

John the Baptist was quizzed: 'Who are you?' (1:19). Just who was John the Baptist? He knew who he was not (1:8, 19, 19–27) and by understanding his own role John was able to point to Jesus.

We know we are insignificant figures in world history but these same questions often come to us too. Why was I born? How should I live? What is the ultimate purpose of my existence? Who am I? John's answers can help us understand something of our own identity.

First, he was not the light but was a witness to the Light (1:7–9). He was the first human witness to the Light with the specific purpose that 'all might believe through him'. 'Believing' is one of the most important words in this gospel (3:16; 6:28–29) and indeed was the ultimate purpose of writing the gospel (20:31). We cannot miss the message that, whatever else we may do in life, nothing is more important than believing in Jesus; and when we do believe nothing is more important than witnessing to Jesus.

John was self-effacing. 'I am not the light' and 'I am not worthy even to untie the thong of his sandal' (1:8, 27). Yet John also suggests that we should not downgrade our unique destiny and task. The Baptist calls us to a way of life, that of being a witness.

Second, John knew that he was not the Messiah, nor Elijah, nor the promised prophet (1:19–24). The Jewish leaders were intrigued by what John was doing and amazed at the popular response to his message. By what right did he preach? Even more, for what reason and on whose authority did he baptise people in the river Jordan, the first crossing of which loomed so large in the nation's history? Just what did he mean by declaring that all Israel needed to repent?

Their question to John was hauntingly simple: 'Who are you?' He made it crystal clear that he was not the Messiah, the Anointed One who would deliver Israel (1:20). That in itself is worth reflecting on: by saying 'I am not the Christ' John shows his eminence because for anyone else to say this would be laughable.[5] John was not the Messiah.

Nor was he Elijah, who was expected to reappear immediately before the coming of the Day of the Lord (see Malachi 4:5–6). However, Jesus affirmed that John *was* Elijah (Matthew 11:13–14; 17:12–13). This is not really a contradiction. John said he was not Elijah and in his own mind this was the absolute truth. Jesus gave a different judgement—John *was* Elijah. We do not always know the whole truth about ourselves. As CFD Moule observed: 'The Baptist humbly rejects the exalted title, but Jesus, on the contrary, bestows it on him. Why should not the two both be correct?'[6]

If not Elijah, then who? The probing continued. Was John 'the prophet'? Deuteronomy 18:15 had promised a future prophet who would be like Moses. John's answer is an abrupt, 'No!' His answers have become sharper and shorter, like a modern politician being quizzed by the media. Both questions reveal that there was much confusion and uncertainty among Jews in those days about expectations of the coming of the Messiah. How could they know when the Messiah would come?

The emissaries from Jerusalem began to panic. Their task to discover the identity of John was failing and their questions revealed a mounting anxiety to gain some sort of control. What was happening could not be fitted into Jewish expectations: 'God is the giver of gifts surpassing the previous religious imagination of Israel'.[7] They had to say something to their superiors! Simply reporting that John was not claiming to be the Messiah, nor Elijah, nor Moses' prophet could scarcely satisfy their religious masters. 'We have to give an official report. Tell us, please: "Who are you?"'

John knew quite clearly who he was (1:6–7, 22–28). First, he was 'a man sent by God' (1:6). This sense of mission permeates the whole gospel; and the first human to know that Jesus was sent from God was John the Baptist.

Second, John also knew that he had been sent as a witness. John is called to *be* a witness and to *bear* witness. The basic idea of a witness carries the legal implication of responsibility and trust. John tells the truth, the whole truth and nothing but the truth about Jesus. He is 'the Lamb of God who takes away the sin of the world' (1:29, 36) and he is the 'Son of God' (1:34). For John, all faith is a response to witness.

Third, John knew that he was called to be a voice of God calling for repentance (1:23). Many Christians have sensed something of what John felt as he was propelled into this special ministry. The great African–American preacher James Earl Massey was a young man of sixteen when he felt such a call:

> I found myself being captured by the spirit of the worship occasion. As I honoured the meaning of the worship hour and opened myself to God, I felt caught up into an

almost transfixed state, and I heard a Voice speaking within my consciousness: 'I want you to preach!' ... The Voice that called me was so clear, and its bidding, though gentle, bore the unmistakable authority of a higher realm.[8]

When the world today is almost overwhelmed by so many voices competing for attention and demanding our commitment, we need to hear—and ourselves embody—the voice of Christ in our world. In our sin we are very deaf. Christ can break through into our lives if only we will listen for that voice.

John called on his hearers to be baptised. Down in the river they joined the community of the prepared, those awaiting the coming of the King. However, in John's gospel he is not so much John the Baptist as John the Witness.

John was also a visionary. He insisted that his baptism was only in the muddy waters of the Jordan whereas the coming one would baptise with the Spirit. His vision was of that one on whom the Spirit would remain, the one who would baptise with the Holy Spirit. This was an important witness because the Messiah—it had been prophesied—would be characterised by full and permanent possession of the Spirit (see Isaiah 11:2, 61:1).

John gave his climactic witness: 'This is the Son of God' (1:34). It would be a long and difficult journey for Jesus before he heard Thomas make the same assertion: 'My Lord and my God' (20:28). Believers of all ages are identified by the same confession of faith.

JOHN PROCLAIMED CHRIST AS THE LAMB OF GOD

There was another significant affirmation made by John: Jesus was hailed as 'the Lamb of God who takes away the sin of the world' (1:29, 36). This image is greatly loved although the precise meaning is not altogether clear.

In what sense is Jesus the Lamb of God? One possible interpretation is to link the sacrifice of Jesus and the lamb sacrificed at the feast of the Passover. A second and more likely interpretation is to see Jesus as the 'lamb that is led to the slaughter'

(Isaiah 53:7; Acts 8:32–35). Some want to link it with the lamb offered in daily sacrifices in the temple, although it is never called 'the lamb of God'.

Yet another suggestion is to relate it to the idea of the scapegoat in the Old Testament (Leviticus 16), but although this certainly may be linked with the idea of bearing away sin, the sacrifice was not of a lamb but of a goat. One other possibility favoured by many modern interpreters is to link it with the image of the triumphant Lamb of God depicted in Revelation (5:6–14).

When serious interpreters are not quite sure, we may be inclined to suggest that it is such a rich image that it conveys something of all these ideas. However, the main emphasis here is unambiguous. This Lamb bears away 'the sin of the world', not individual sins as such, but that sin which is inherent in all humanity. As Hoskyns summarised: 'Jesus bears the consequence of human sin in order that its guilt may be removed'.[9]

Moreover, John insisted that this one who came after him in time was in fact before him (1:30). This Word is also 'from the span of space and time'.[10] This was not a case of knowing *who* Jesus was but of knowing *what* Jesus was.

The Isenheim Altarpiece by Gruenewald is one of the most famous religious artworks of all time. The centre panel depicts a tortured Christ on the cross. Immediately to the right, standing off to the side, is John the Baptist holding open a copy of the Scriptures and pointing to the figure on the cross. At John's feet is a small lamb. This is what John's gospel tells us about John the Baptist: he points to Jesus who is the Lamb of God that takes away the sin of the world.

This stands as a reminder to us that if we want to be faithful disciples of Jesus we need to be willing to be a voice—a witness. Like John we are called to know our place, to know our time and to speak God's word to our situation. Our otherwise unremarkable lives can become a voice that points others to Jesus.

The encounter between John and Jesus has prompted several questions. Can we live so as to light up others' lives? How will we answer the same questions that

John had to face? Who are you? Why do you live like this? Why do you do these strange things?

Can we respond with the affirmation which is also our ambition: 'I am a witness, a voice for the living God, and hope above all else to point others to Jesus'?

Questions for discussion

1. We sometimes speak about the struggle for identity in young (and older) people. Explore ways in which this study of John the Baptist and Jesus helps us with this issue.

2. In what sense is John 'the perfect prototype of the true evangelist'?

3. Discuss the similarities and differences between the preaching of John the Baptist and Jesus. How does this guide us in our mission today?

4. How important is it to know who I am not, as well as who I am?

5. Explore the whole question of being a witness for Jesus in modern society. What do you find hard in witnessing and what encouragements can you share with others?

6. Have you known people whom you believe were sent by God to you? Have you sensed that you were such a sent person for another? How can we know when we are truly sent by God?

7. Discuss the quotation in which James Earl Massey recalled his call to preach. Have you ever sensed such a distinct call? How important are such experiences?

8. What do you find the most convincing interpretation of Jesus as 'the Lamb of God who bears away the sin of the world'?

9. If possible, download a reproduction of the Isenheim Altarpiece by Gruenewald and discuss what it means for you.

Further along the way

1. B Leonard, 'Pursuing the Prophetic', sermon dated 16 January 2011 <http:/day1.org/signup> accessed 16/8/16.

2. T Kelly, *A Testament of Devotion* (London: Hodder and Stoughton, 1961), p. 107.

3. H Hesse, *The Glass Bead Game* (London: Vintage: 2000 [1970]), p. 464.

4. W Wink, as quoted by FD Bruner, *The Gospel of John. A Commentary* (Grand Rapids: Eerdmans, 2012), p. 62.

5. A Schlatter, as quoted by Bruner, *The Gospel of John*, p. 61.

6. CFD Moule, *The Phenomenon of the New Testament* (London: SCM, 1967), p. 70.

7. AJ Kelly and FJ Moloney, *Experiencing God in the Gospel of John* (Paulist Press: New York, 2003), p. 66.

8. T George, 'James Earl Massey: Steward of the Story', http//www.firstthings.com./web-exclusives/2016/07/, accessed 25/7/16.

9. EC Hoskyns, *The Fourth Gospel* (ed. FN Davey; London: Faber & Faber, 1947), p. 176.

10. Kelly and Moloney, *Experiencing God*, p. 51.

'Christ Driving the Traders from the Temple', El Greco, 1571–76

CHAPTER TWO

IN MY FATHER'S HOUSE: JESUS AND THE LOAN SHARKS
(JOHN 2:13–25)

To call these unnamed men 'loan sharks', as Eugene Peterson does in his paraphrase *The Message,* may be somewhat unfair. That they incurred the wrath of Jesus is clear. Although they were not the only ones who came under his condemnation on that fateful day in the Jerusalem temple, they are central to the story. Obviously these 'moneychangers' (which is the more literal translation of the word in 2:14) were very unhappy to meet this strange prophet from Galilee. This was an encounter with Jesus that was unwelcome, confusing and challenging.

Who were these men with all these coins in the temple? Why was Jesus there and why did he act in this way? We find it hard to imagine Jesus as being angry. So why was Jesus so angry? These questions are central to this story.

WHY DID JESUS GO UP TO THE TEMPLE AT JERUSALEM? (JOHN 2:13–16)

We are told that Jesus went *up* to Jerusalem. Everyone had to go *up* to that famed city because it was built on a mountain named Mount Zion, the fabled location that for the Psalmist and in Christian devotion became the city of God (Psalm 48; Hebrews 12:22; Revelation 14:1).

Why did Jesus go to Jerusalem? Evidently Jesus found many followers in the country around Galilee; he could have continued indefinitely away from Jerusalem and enjoyed the company of his mother and brothers (2:12). We picture him addressing crowds on the hills where he was welcomed and generally fêted. Why bother with that great metropolis with all its scheming politics, its display of cruel Roman military power, its noisy crowds, its corrupt religious leaders, and its physical and moral dangers? Some Jews in his day had given the whole lot away and settled into community life near the Dead Sea where they meditated and prayed and cut themselves off from the temple and all its corruption.

But no, Jesus went to Jerusalem and the temple. He went there because he was a devout Jew. He brought his message *to* Jerusalem, not *against* Jerusalem. The temple was the focus of Jewish religious, national and social identity. Although Jews affirmed that God was not confined to a temple made with hands, they believed God had chosen to dwell in this place, in its Holy of Holies; and, in its ritual, God was to be found.

Jesus had been to the temple before, possibly many times. He had been thought lost there as a young man and had asked his worried parents why they had not expected to find him in what he called 'my Father's house' (Luke 2:49). This of course is how Jesus also refers to the temple in this story (2:16). This sense of intimacy with the Father is a decisive clue to Jesus' own sense of identity and helps us explain the anger he felt when he saw what was happening in that sacred space.

Jesus must have been impressed, even overwhelmed, by that huge complex. Today, part of the retaining wall of that Temple—the 'wailing wall'—is the last surviving remnant of that Jewish world and still attracts Jewish devotion and prayer. That magnificent building had taken decades to construct and was still not finished in Jesus' day. In the Holy of Holies every inch of wall surface was overlaid with gold. Jewish historian Josephus claimed that after the sack of Jerusalem in 70 CE gold from the temple flooded the market, so much so that the standard of gold was depreciated to half its former value.

This was Passover week and the city was crowded. This remembrance of the delivery of the Jewish people in Egypt was central to Jewish faith. Josephus improbably claimed that two and a half million Jews came each year for that festival. At Passover every family had to sacrifice a lamb, so the city was jammed with bleating sheep—someone has calculated that as many as 255,600 lambs were sacrificed. Lambs could be bought in the temple portico. Imagine the scene. Thousands were crammed into the city. The smell of burning meat and heady incense wafted across the city. Trumpet blasts announced prayers and sacrifices—everything was focused on the Temple, nervously overlooked by Roman soldiers from the Antonia fortress.

Little wonder that artists have been captivated by the drama of this scene! Jesus walked into the colonnaded Royal Portico, the bustling, colourful, crowded centre of Jewish life. Here pilgrims gathered to organise accommodation, meet friends, change money to pay their temple tax and to buy lambs, doves or—for the rich—oxen. This was not in the inner courts but the most accessible and public section of the large complex, designed to serve like a forum. This was all necessary for the temple's work to proceed. Note that John uses two words for 'temple' here. The first (2:14) refers to this outer complex but the second relates to the inner sanctuary, the Holy of Holies (2:19–21).

So Jesus went to the temple as a devout Jew, a solitary figure in that vast crowd, intending to worship along with so many other faithful pilgrims.

WHY DID JESUS ACT AS HE DID? (2:14–16)

Jesus had been there previously but he had never acted like this before. The story is briefly told but captures our imagination. With a simple kind of hastily fashioned whip (probably from the rushes that were there for animal feed) he herded the animals out of that space, tipped over the tables piled high with coins and then forced the dove sellers to take their cages away as he uttered one emphatic command—'Stop making my Father's house a marketplace' or 'shopping mall' (*The Message*). Animals bellowing, bleating and panicking—coins rolling noisily—startled traders and customers scrambling to rescue what they could from the chaos—what a scene! It was probably all over in a couple of minutes.

What had he done and why? His demonstration obviously attracted attention but not enough to warrant any intervention by temple guards or Roman soldiers, such as happened when Paul visited the temple (Acts 21).

The other three gospels place this story during the last week of Jesus' life and it became the trigger that activated his arrest (Matthew 21:12–17; Mark 11:15–19; Luke 19:45–48). But John places it here, right near the beginning. Theoretically it could have happened twice, although that seems unlikely. In John it serves an identical theological function as in the Synoptics since the opposition to Jesus by the 'Jews' is first revealed in this incident and the path to the cross became inevitable.

What made Jesus do this? On any reading he was hopping mad with what he saw there. This is not 'Gentle Jesus, meek and mild'! As William Willimon observes: 'If all you know about Jesus is that he is kind to children and considers the lilies, you've got another think coming'.[1] Surely it was the blazing anger of Jesus, not a thin whip (only mentioned in John's account) that cleared and cleansed the temple.

We need to stop here for a moment. Jesus was really angry. It was not the only time he was angry. Mark 3:5 records that Jesus was angry with those stupid legalists who queried whether it was lawful to heal a man on the Sabbath and 'he was grieved at their hardness of heart'. So here, too, Jesus was angry. It was a moral power. His blazing anger—not the flimsy whips—startled all those who were there. After all, the Old Testament often speaks about God's anger against sin and the failures of his people. Whilst this can be interpreted in primitive ways, the wrath of God is always the flip side of love, the anguished response to the wilful disobedience of a faithless people.

One who does not feel anger in some situations is less than human. Simply to say the word 'Holocaust' or talk about child abuse is to explain what I mean. There is a righteous anger at all that destroys or cripples others.

Of course much anger can be destructive and deadly. Pathological anger leads to murder and vicious crimes. There is good sense behind the traditional listing of 'anger' as one of the seven deadly sins. Even in the church all too often we encounter an unhealthy anger. We angrily condemn those with whom we disagree and are quick to label others. American novelist Ann Lamott wrote: 'You can safely assume you've created God in your own image when it turns out that God hates all the same people you do'.[2]

But the anger evidenced by Jesus in this story is of a different order. It is right to be angry about injustice and oppression. As a bumper sticker says: 'If you're not outraged, you're not paying attention'. We do well, however, to recall the wise caution of John Oman—'To be a peacemaker one must fight in peace as well as for it'.[3]

So, here is the crux: just why did Jesus act in this way? In what way was the anger of Jesus advancing his work of love? CS Lewis once linked anger with love:

> Anger—no peevish fit of temper, but just generous, scalding indignation—passes (not necessarily at once) into embracing, exultant, re-welcoming love. That is how friends and lovers are truly reconciled. Hot wrath, hot love. Such anger is the fluid that love bleeds when you cut it.[4]

Still, why not instead turn over the tables of the crooked and corrupt tax collectors? Why not try to drive out people from the pagan temples? Why such a scene in the house of God?

Many diverse and speculative answers have been given. We should begin with the recognition that Jesus was acting just as many earlier prophets had when they performed symbolic acts that challenged the established religion of the day. Hebrew Bible predictions included Malachi 3:1: 'the Lord whom you seek will suddenly come to his temple … and he will purify …', whilst Zechariah 14 prophesied about all nations going to Jerusalem to worship (which they could do in the temple precincts, open to 'all nations'). But they go to pray not to bargain: 'there shall no longer be a trader in the house of the Lord of hosts on that day' (14:21). In other words, Jesus protested not against the corruptions, but against the very presence of traders there. Mark when he tells the story links it with Isaiah and Jeremiah: 'My house shall be called a house of prayer for all the nations, but you have made it a den of robbers' (11:17).

FC Hoskyns has comprehensively suggested: 'The action of Jesus is not merely that of a Jewish reformer: it is a sign of the advent of the Messiah; it is not merely a protest against the irreverence and corruption of Jewish worship; it is a sign that the end of animal sacrifice is at hand'.[5]

The temple was not now a welcoming open house of a loving Father but a market place where profits were made. God is against that external religion which is concerned with prestige, power, privilege, politics, protocol and precedent. These are the tables that Jesus always overturns. The Church father Origen, who usually found an allegorical meaning in Scripture, wrote: 'Jesus overturns the tables in the souls of those fond of money'.[6] As so often, his interpretation is extraordinarily apt.

Eventually in Jerusalem this confrontation led to Jesus' death. All the evil of the world as embodied in that system crucified him. Jesus was crucified precisely because he moved from Galilee to Jerusalem. This was not an act of civil disobedience but of a holy obedience.

JESUS TAUGHT THE MONEYCHANGERS AND HIS DISCIPLES A PROFOUND LESSON IN THE TEMPLE (2:17–22)

The moneychangers do not appear again in the story. We can only imagine what their response was to all that had happened. Did some become followers of this strong prophet from Galilee? John does add that many believed in his name during that Passover festival because they saw 'the signs that he was doing' (2:23). The moneychangers certainly saw that 'sign' at first hand. We would like to think that some moneychangers were among that group of new disciples.

Had they been startled into an awareness of what they had been doing? The excuse that 'everybody is doing it' still recurs today. Was there some buried half-consciousness, or at least a suspicion, that what they were doing was wrong? Was that why no one really tackled Jesus when it happened? Were some bystanders quietly cheering what they saw? After all, Jesus did not attack any of the people who were using the moneychangers. The sellers of doves for the poor people were judged for where they were selling, not because they were doing it.

We cannot know the answers to these questions, although it is to be stressed that what the moneychangers were doing was not wrong as such. Ancient as well as modern travellers need the services of money exchanges. People needed to change the currency they used in the markets for the Tyrian coins that carried no effigy and so were necessary for use in temple business. The business had to be done. Perhaps some charged too high a fee for the exchange but there is no evidence that they did. It was a necessary service. This is not a criticism of business and banks as such for they perform an essential task. It was not so much *what* they were doing but *where* they were doing it. The moneychangers were not condemned by Jesus and his contemporaries in the way that tax collectors were, because the latter both collaborated with the hated Romans and were notorious for the huge personal profits that they pocketed.

Certainly John makes it clear that this 'whip sermon', as FD Bruner calls it, provoked religious controversy.[7] The disciples remembered (2:17, 22*).*

Remembrance is a key role of the disciples in John (see 12:16) for it is a mark of the presence of the Spirit with them. Jesus had promised that the Holy Spirit 'will teach you everything and remind you of all that I have said to you' (14:26).

What did they remember? First, they remembered a psalm which is full of allusions to the Messiah. Psalm 69:21 prophesied: 'for my thirst they gave me vinegar to drink' and then verse 9 stated: 'zeal for your house has consumed me'. The tense in John is changed from past to future: zeal *will* consume me, for this is a prediction of the cross. Zeal for God, a boiling over of enthusiasm for God and his truth, is always dangerous.

The Jews not unreasonably 'answer' Jesus' deed by questioning him: 'Who are you to do this? Can you give us a sign about what you are doing?' These were the wrong questions. They should have been asking: 'How should we respond to this prophetic witness? How can we show our repentance?' But there was too much to be lost by too many.

As so often in John, Jesus' reply is misunderstood, creates confusion and then leads to a clarifying insight that will later strengthen the faith of the church: 'Destroy this temple and in three days I will raise it up'. Of course the incredulous Jews were totally amazed at this extraordinary claim. They thought that Jesus was somehow claiming literally to be able to rebuild their huge stone edifice in three days! After the resurrection the disciples remembered and understood what Jesus was asserting and promising.

Martin Luther proclaimed: 'God has established another temple for his residence: the precious humanity of our lord Jesus Christ. There, and nowhere else, God wants to be found'.[8] The ultimate meaning of the cleansing of the temple is Christological, not ecclesiological—it teaches us about the meaning of Jesus, not about how the temple or the church should be run.

Perhaps here too is the seed of the idea which Paul developed of the church being his body, and that God dwells in the believers as in a holy sanctuary (1 Cor. 3:16). Richard Rohr insists: 'When God is seen as "outside", the sacrificial system will remain. However, when God moves inside, you are the temple and sacrifice is no longer required. The only sacrifice now, is me'.

John is really saying that God's earthly temple will be no more. Instead we will have Jesus as the one in whom we find God. His body is the new location for God's presence on earth. After the resurrection they believed the 'scripture' (no one text is cited) and the word of Jesus (2:22). So may we.

HOW ELSE MAY THIS STORY CHALLENGE US TODAY?

This was not a blanket condemnation against all forms of fund raising and commercial transactions on church property, as I used sometimes to hear in my younger days. It is not about an imagined misuse of such spaces, for we do not regard a church building or any other edifice as a temple like that ancient Jewish one. 'God cannot be safely contained in a material building. God is outside the calculated exchanges of any human activity.'[9]

What else may we learn from this story?

Jesus made an effective prophetic criticism from a heart that was pure. Such a prophetic act was the product of prayer and reflection. Here is the model for our prophetic task:

> It does not leap into the prophet's mind and then out his or her mouth without any activity in-between. Nor is it delivered with a whine or a pout, a spirit of 'hurt feelings' that diminishes or destroys its value. Rather it is delivered robustly and unmistakenly, without the ambiguity that is merely reflecting the prophet's personal and disturbed opinions.[10]

Eugene Peterson once observed that his fellow American pastors had become 'a company of shopkeepers': 'They are preoccupied with shopkeepers' concerns—how to get new customers, how to keep the customers happy, how to lure customers away from competitors down the street'.[11]

That is not just an American problem! And it is not just a pastor's problem. The challenge is to *respect* God in all that we do. The so-called 'prosperity gospel', in which faith is proclaimed as a guarantee of material blessings, is also surely condemned by this story.

Can we go more deeply? When the church is at the heart of the establishment, colluding with greedy powers, its leaders at home in the seats of power whilst the common people suffer from poverty and hardship, is not this still agonising for Jesus? Is not this what always happens when religion as a system replaces the prophet from Galilee?

Archbishop Rowan Williams reflected on this passage:

> When Jesus has cleared out the temple, when he has thrown out those people involved in manufacturing religion, there he stands with his friends in a great silence and a great space. And he says: this is the space where all people may feel at home; this is a space large enough for all to come because this is where God lives. This is where God is at home, and this is where all human beings may be at home.[12]

Tim Costello, formerly CEO of World Vision Australia, has cited the liturgy that he and his staff prayed each week. Here is a prayer for anger, the kind of anger that Jesus showed in the temple. It contains the refrain:

> Solo Voice: May God bless us with anger ...
>
> All: Anger at injustice, oppression, and exploitation of people and our earth; so that we may work for justice, freedom, and peace.[13]

Questions for discussion

1. Why was Jesus so angry with the moneychangers? How can we distinguish between 'good' and 'bad' anger in our lives?

2. Can you identify any contemporary practices in the church today that might justify the kind of condemnation that Jesus gave to those in the temple on that fateful day?

3. Discuss the quotation from William Willimon: 'If all you know about Jesus is that he is kind to children and considers the lilies, you've got another think coming'.

4. Read and discuss the quotation from CS Lewis in which he links anger and love.

5. 'The ultimate meaning of the cleansing of the temple is Christological, not ecclesiological: it teaches us about the meaning of Jesus, not about how the temple/church should be run.' Is this how you understand the meaning of this story?

6. Are there issues about which we should be manifesting a prophetic anger? What can we do about this?

7. Can you think of times, as the World Vision staff do, when we should pray for anger?

1. W Willimon, *Pulpit Resource*, January to March 2001, pp. 41–42.
2. A Lamott, *Travelling Mercies. Some thoughts on Faith* (New York: Random House, 1999), p. 22.
3. For details of his teaching, see J Oman, *The War and its Issues* (Cambridge: Cambridge University Press, 1915).
4. CS Lewis, *Letters to Malcolm: Chiefly on Prayer* (London: Collins, 1966), p. 98.
5. FC Hoskyns, *The Fourth Gospel* (London: Faber and Faber, 1947), p. 194.
6. Origen, as quoted by FD Bruner, *The Gospel of John. A Commentary* (Grand Rapids: Eerdmans, 2012), p. 149.
7. Bruner, *The Gospel of John*, p. 142.
8. Luther, as quoted by Bruner, *The Gospel of John*, p. 142.
9. AJ Kelly and FJ Moloney, *Experiencing God in the Gospel of John* (New York: Paulist Press, 2003), p. 92.
10. JG Sobosan, *Christian Commitment and Prophetic Living* (Mystic, Conn.: Twenty-Third Publications, 1986), p. 66.
11. E Peterson, *Working the Angles. The Shape of Pastoral Integrity* (Grand Rapids: Eerdmans, 1987), p. 1.
12. Sermon by Archbishop Rowan William at St Paul's 'Within the Walls', Rome (11 March 2012) www.archbishopofcanterbury.org/ ... /archbishopssermons at st paul's within the walls, accessed 16 August 2016.
13. T Costello, *Faith* (Melbourne: Hardie Grant, 2016), p. 263.

'Christ Healing', Carl Bloch, 1875

CHAPTER THREE

LONG-DISTANCE FAITH: JESUS AND A WORRIED FATHER
(JOHN 4:43-54)

They say that 'absence makes the heart grow fonder'. That may well be true but there can be no doubt that distance makes anxiety about a family crisis even more intense. This story comes from ancient times when communications were basic, but the emotion and stress of this father still resonates with anyone who has had to face a similar crisis. His loved son was seriously sick and close to death. His anxiety was intensified by the fact that he was in Cana and his son was over twenty kilometres away in Capernaum. The crisis was immediate. What could he possibly do? He asked Jesus to help.

A couple of years ago my wife and I were in Scotland when we received news that our younger grandson in Melbourne was seriously ill. He had collapsed in a coma and had been rushed to the Children's Hospital. We had access to modern communications, but even so we felt helpless and were of course terribly distressed. What could we do? It was Easter Sunday morning when we heard the news and we worshipped at the historic St Giles' Cathedral in Edinburgh. The one thing we could do was to ask God to help. That was what we did but we keenly felt the distance that separated us from our sick and greatly loved grandson. He was diagnosed with Type 1 Diabetes, and though burdened with that illness he is now a happy and active youth. Certainly he was surrounded by many prayers and was cared for in one of the best children's hospitals in the world. We think that our prayers were answered, not least by the provision of a dedicated and skilled staff.

This is one New Testament story where despite the great divides of time and place we can immediately identify with the emotion and anxiety of a parent for a child. The question for us is whether we have the same kind of persevering faith that the father showed and which helped bring the deliverance of his son. We can be helped as we read this story with honesty and imagination. The fundamental question to discover is just who this Jesus was who could do such wonderful things.

JESUS CAME TO HIS OWN COUNTRY (JOHN 4:43–46)

Whenever we read a story in John's Gospel it is important to examine closely the way in which it is linked to the previous section. The greater part of John 4 is devoted to the encounter between Jesus and the Samaritan woman which led to her faith and then to many in her community also believing.[1] John is careful to emphasise that although the witness of the unnamed woman was significant, these villagers believed because of the word of Jesus (4:41). This led them to confess that Jesus truly is 'the Saviour of the world' (4:42).

John then reports that Jesus came from Samaria to Galilee and in fact to Cana, where, as John reminds us, Jesus had changed water into wine (4:43–46). There is, however, one comment that we need to consider carefully: 'Jesus himself had testified that a prophet has no honour in the prophet's own country'. This is normally understood to relate to Galilee from where Jesus came. There is no doubt that in the other gospels this epigram is directly linked with Galilee (see Mark 6:1–6; Matthew 13:54–58; Luke 4:16–20). However, John rather confusingly affirms that when Jesus came to Galilee the locals welcomed him since they had seen all that he had done in Jerusalem at festival time (4:45). What had he done that so attracted these Galileans? As John recorded, many had 'believed in his name' because of the numerous signs that Jesus had done (2:23). These 'signs' are not described in John.

The welcome of these Galileans does not seem to follow logically the quotation about a prophet without honour. Some scholars have noted that there are other possibilities—perhaps Judea as a whole or Jerusalem was meant. After all, as Hoskyns notes, Jerusalem was 'the home of every Jew' and that was where the rejection of the Galilean prophet was to be so dramatically completed.[2] But John may mean us to understand that the welcome of the Galileans was superficial, that theirs was the kind of faith that he rebuked: 'Unless you see signs and wonders you will not believe' (4:48).

The tradition certainly links the saying with Galilee, but the most important point is that Jesus was rejected precisely in the place where he might have hoped for acceptance and affirmation. Indeed, we have previously been told that when the eternal Word came into the world 'even his own people did not accept him' (1:11). This tragic response lies behind the critical way in which John refers to 'the Jews' throughout his gospel, a theme which we will discuss in a later chapter.[3]

This rejection, this failure to give honour and welcome to a 'home town hero', is what Australians tend to describe as 'the tall poppy syndrome'. It must have hurt Jesus as it would anyone who acquires some renown outside his or her immediate environment. Moreover, as a later study will explore, the relationship between Jesus and his own earthly family—his mother and brothers—shows that here too he was not given the respect and support he could well have expected. Because many were familiar with Jesus and his earthly family they did not listen to him objectively. They were prejudiced. Why? Because he had lived among them— they could not hear his message.

'Familiarity breeds contempt'. There is something about familiarity that changes the way we respond to others. We tend to think differently about people we don't know well. It can be easier for these people to shape their reputations and position themselves as authorities. On the other hand, it can be easy to feel differently about the people we know. Why? We know more about them. We think of them just as ordinary people—not 'experts'.

The greater the space and time between the presence of an especially gifted person and the average person, the easier it becomes for the average person to acknowledge the other's gifts without being made to feel inferior or worthless in comparison. Van Gogh managed to sell only one painting in his lifetime, yet his paintings now sell for millions of dollars. Many Christian leaders across the centuries have experienced similar frustrations in their own lifetimes.

How do we look at the people around us? Is it possible that God actually can be speaking through them? Could they have insights that would be helpful to us? Are we ignoring the people we know? We need to be careful not to ignore someone just because we know them. The church is meant to be a community that recognises gifts and affirms each believer so that no prophet or any other person should be without honour in his or her own church.

THE OFFICIAL AND HIS SICK SON (JOHN 4:46–50)

The man is not named but is described as 'a royal official', which most probably means that he was employed by Herod Antipas (who was not strictly a king but was of the royal house and exercised actual rule in Judea). It is not clear whether this official was a Jew or a Gentile; if he was not a Jew this marks a complete illustration of the spread of the message of Jesus, from Jew to Samaritan and now to a Gentile. Whatever the official may have been, Herod was not popular with the Jewish people, so this official may not have been acceptable to many who were in Cana.

None of this really mattered to this unnamed man. His son was 'at the point of death' and he was far from home. But he had heard about Jesus and what he had been doing and so he dropped all protocol (such as an official might have commanded) and begged Jesus 'to come down and heal his son' (4:47). Capernaum was indeed 'down', some 230 metres down on the shore of the lake.

So we know that the man believed that Jesus could heal his son. If only he could persuade him to be there in time, his boy would live.

The response of Jesus seems to rebuke the man: 'Unless you see signs and wonders you will not believe' (4:48). However, the 'you' in this remark is plural: 'Unless you, all of you, see signs … '. The challenge of Jesus was not only to the official but to the wider community of Jews who were amazed at what Jesus did (and solely for that reason wanted to follow him). Still, the official could well have interpreted these words as a refusal from Jesus, especially when Jesus made no move to race down to Capernaum.

But the official did not give up. He repeated his request and then Jesus simply declared: 'Your son lives' (4:49–50). The official heard this and promptly started on his journey home, believing what Jesus had said. He simply believed 'the word that Jesus spoke to him'. The word gives life as John has told us (1:4).

The pattern of this 'sign' in Cana (4:54) is similar to the first sign in Cana. In both stories there is: (1) the expression of need; (2) seeming resistance from Jesus; (3) faith in his power persisting; (4) Jesus dealing with the matter in a manner different from what is requested or expected; (5) servants participating in the action; (6) some sort of faith resulting.[4] Asking is important in this gospel. The man asks a second time and Jesus responds with the healing word of life. That is why Luther called this story 'a beautiful example of faith'.[5]

JESUS SPEAKS THE WORD OF LIFE AND PERFORMS A SIGN

What is unusual in this story is what might be called the 'long-distance' healing. A somewhat similar story is recorded by Matthew when a centurion's servant is also healed at a distance by Jesus (Matthew 8:5–13 // Luke 7:2–10). For John the crucial factor is his emphasis on the official believing that the word of Jesus alone had the power to bring healing. The power of Jesus is not confined to his bodily presence. Faith in the word is sufficient. This of course has relevance for later readers like us who cannot see Jesus in the flesh but are invited to have faith in his word.

We sometimes imagine that if only we had been there—back in that day—it would have been easier for us to believe. But it is not so. Many who saw him actually perform remarkable healings and heard his matchless words did not believe. Even though we are at a distance we can still hear the word of Jesus. As Craddock puts it: 'Because of the presence of the word in the church ours is not a religion of then and there but here and now ... It is difficult to imagine a point more vital to the life of the church than this'.[6]

The story makes it clear that the power of the word was instantaneous (4:51–53). The timing was exact. The boy was healed at the very moment that Jesus had spoken the healing word of promise: 'Your son lives'.

What seems to be important is that Jesus in the gospel of John does not reject the miraculous as such but does resist any *demand* for a miraculous sign and wonder. Some who still demand that God performs 'signs and wonders' so that they can believe seem to have missed this most vital insight of John.

Of course we still pray for healing for loved ones. Sometimes it is hard to know that God hears and answers. I remember the story told in the 'Granny' column of *The Sydney Morning Herald* some years ago. A young boy had dialled the telephone prayer line that some Christians ran but was dismayed when the line went dead. He told his parents that he was disappointed that 'God had hung up on him'. But I also remember how William Temple, one-time Archbishop of Canterbury and a great theologian, remarked that when he prayed coincidences happened but when he did not pray the coincidences stopped. However we may want to analyse the phenomenon, believers in every age have discovered that God hears and answers the prayers of his people. As Temple has also written: 'For though faith is always met with blessing from God, that blessing does not always take the desired or expressed form, as in this case it did'.[7]

John is careful to tell us that this healing was what he called 'the second sign that Jesus did after coming from Judea to Galilee' (4:54). The first was the miracle at the wedding (2:11). Signs are of great importance in John; indeed John's gospel has been interpreted as 'A Book of Signs'. There are six special signs that John emphasises and these give structure to his account: see 2:1–12; 4:46–54; 5:1–9; 6:1–14; 9:1–12; 11:1–44. Some prefer to speak of seven signs, regarding the resurrection itself as a seventh sign. Some of these signs we will be discussing in later chapters. The signs are the basis of belief for John's readers (20:30–31).

The word 'sign' has a somewhat special meaning in John—it signifies an event which manifests 'the glory of God'. A 'sign' is something that is not simply miraculous but also reveals Jesus' divine nature and mission to those who are open to seeing it. The sign has a theological importance because it points to something beyond itself. In John every miracle is a sign to the underlying great miracle of the incarnation. If we believe that God became human—or, in John's language, that 'the Word became flesh'—then belief in the miracles of Jesus becomes entirely consistent.

Just as the witness of the Samaritan led to her community coming to faith we must note the impact of this healing story: 'So he himself believed, along with his whole household' (4:53). This sounds like many of the responses to the gospel that we find in Acts where households were converted (for example, Acts 16:25–34). Moloney observes that in the wedding miracle the disciples believed in him (2:11) and now here the officer's persistent faith leads others to faith as well.[8] The servants who had seen the recovery of the son and gone to tell the father are also impelled to faith. Both miracle stories show that faith in this gospel is not only a personal commitment to the word of Jesus but leads others to faith as well. Authentic belief always has a missionary function.

The question remains for us to examine whether we have read the signs for ourselves. A relationship can be destroyed if one partner does not correctly read the signs that are being given by the other. The traveller who misreads a road sign can end up lost and lonely. We still often look for signs. Signs of whether or not to take a job, to enter into a relationship, to decide upon one course over another, to

Further along the way

continue treatment or give in to the inevitability of a diagnosis, to keep faith with another or betray that relationship. At one point or another, we all look for signs, something that will help us to find the way, or at least find the next step forward.

The more significant 'signs' for living, however, are offered in the gospel stories of Jesus. As we study these signs in John's Gospel we can discover the reality of what the signs promise, a living relationship with Jesus the Son of God and Saviour of the world. Don't miss the signs!

Questions for discussion

1. Discuss the plight of the worried father. Imagine the anguish he felt. Are there any parallel experiences that you have known when distance added to your anxiety? In what ways may we still look to Jesus for help?

2. Explore how Jesus must have felt when his own family and people rejected him. Have you ever felt like that? Can you think of any modern examples of this rejection? How can we give honour to 'prophets' in our community?

3. Why did Luther call his story 'a beautiful example of faith'? What were the main characteristics of this man's faith? How can we cultivate a similar faith?

4. Discuss the quotation from Craddock: 'Because of the presence of the word in the church ours is not a religion of then and there but here and now'.

5. Compare this story with the one in Matthew 8:5–13. What are the similarities and differences?

6. What do you think about this observation from William Temple, that when he prayed coincidences happened but when he did not pray the coincidences stopped. Have you had any similar experiences?

7. 'Authentic belief always has a missionary function'. Discuss what this means, and do you think it is still true today?

8. Explore the meaning of 'sign' in John's gospel. Look briefly at the signs in John (2:1–12; 4:46–54; 5:1–9; 6:1–14; 9:1–12; 11:1–44) and think about what each sign reveals.

Further along the way

1. See the discussion in KR Manley, *On the Way to Faith* (Macquarie Park: Morling Press, 2013), pp. 30–37.

2. EC Hoskyns, *The Fourth Gospel* (London: Faber and Faber, 1947), p. 260.

3. See Chapter 7 below.

4. B Witherington III, *John's Wisdom. A Commentary on the Fourth Gospel* (Louisville, KY: Westminster John Knox Press, 1995), p. 127.

5. Luther, as quoted by FD Bruner, *The Gospel of John: A Commentary* (Grand Rapids: Eerdmans, 2012), p. 286.

6. FB Craddock, *John* (Atlanta: John Knox Press, 1982), p. 41.

7. W Temple, *Readings in St John's Gospel* (London: Macmillan, 1961), p. 71.

8. FJ Moloney, *The Gospel of John* (Sacra Pagina 4: Collegeville, Minn.: Liturgical Press, 1998), pp. 154–55.

'Healing of the Blind Man', Duccio di Buoninsegna, 1308–11

CHAPTER FOUR

DO YOU WANT TO BE MADE WELL? JESUS AND THE DISABLED MAN
(JOHN 5:1–18)

Our media-savvy generation knows that timing is everything. If you are launching a new product then when you announce it is significant. Some years ago the Australian Labor Party, after long decades of being in the political wilderness, had huge success with its slogan: 'It's Time!'

Jesus did not have any such strategic advisors but there can be little doubt that his timing was always right. This story shows us how Jesus came as divine healer at the right time and to the right place. So, as we read about a man who had been paralysed, depressed and defeated for thirty-eight years—lying by a pool of false promise and of endless empty waiting that always failed him—this moment of healing and hope came just in time. From the disabled man's perspective one more day was one too long. But why did Jesus heal him on a sabbath? What was the point of that timing?

Once again Jesus had gone up to Jerusalem for a festival of the Jews, although we are not told which feast this one was. Jesus regularly celebrated with his people although it is the sabbath that is crucial to this story. It is significant that Jesus did not simply stay in the sacred space of the temple but went to be where the smelly, the unclean and the needy gathered beside the pool. That is always the way of Jesus—to look for the desperate and needy.

We might be tempted to ask, why on earth did Jesus heal this man on the sabbath? He was a devout Jew and knew the laws that distinguished his people. Preeminent amongst these was keeping the sabbath. Why didn't Jesus whisper to the man: 'Be here again tomorrow and I will help you'? After thirty-eight years, surely another day was not really important! Why did he do it?

The miracle and the sabbath belong together. Jesus deliberately healed on the sabbath. It was a premeditated provocation so that his true identity might be revealed. All the sign-miracles are totally concerned with Christology—who is this Jesus?

This story is a sign, then, not only of the undeserved grace of God in healing this man, but that he did it on the sabbath is a sign that Jesus is the Son of God. The healing shows *what Jesus does* and the sabbath controversy shows *who Jesus is*. Both belong together. The longer section of the chapter (5:19–47) demonstrates how Jesus defines and defends his relationship with God the Father.

HEALING BY THE POOL IS A SIGN OF GRACE: THIS IS WHAT JESUS DOES (5:1–9)

There is a brief description of exactly where this miracle took place. The 'Sheep Gate' is of course where sheep intended for ritual sacrifice were driven, so it was adjacent to the temple. The pool is given various names in the manuscripts but should probably be called 'Bethesda' (House of Mercy) although some manuscripts have 'Bethzatha' (House of Olives). The site has been identified by archaeologists and is located beneath St Anne's monastery. This was a twin pool 'as large as a football field and about twenty feet deep' with five porticoes, one on each side and one separating the two pools.[1]

Public baths in Hellenistic Roman times were often linked with healing waters and there are echoes of this kind of belief in this story. There is one particular myth alluded to here. Readers will note that modern versions omit verse 4, which records that an angel of the Lord went down at certain seasons into the pool and stirred up the water. Whoever stepped in first after the stirring of the water was made whole. One had to become wet in order to be made well.

Readers should not be confused or alarmed by such a verse being omitted from modern versions. Careful scholarship has examined every manuscript and in a quite scientific way identified which were the earlier and most reliable texts. Gordon Fee details the reasons for omitting this verse and concludes that this story bears the 'earmarks of ancient superstition'.[2] Even so, there is an allusion to this belief in the comment by the invalid when he complains that he has no one to help him 'when the water is stirred up' and so has no chance of healing (5:7).

There is perhaps a suggestion in this story that Jesus was in 'competition' with the ancient healing sanctuaries and displaced the magical qualities associated with this site.[3]

The waters gave a false promise, at least for this poor man. I am reminded of a popular film some years ago named *Cocoon* (1985), a science fiction fantasy comedy in which three old men, one with cancer, dive and play gleefully in a pool that makes them well and restores their youthful strength. The pool's power comes from aliens, but the men must keep the secret from others. When the secret gets out, too many of the 'inferior' types crowd into the pool and its powers are lost. The miracle was only for the few, so the pool was finally a cruel place. This 'competitive healing' is the same as in the stories associated with the pool of Bethesda.[4]

The miracle is a brilliant example of how God comes to us in undeserved grace. Here was a man in pain, alone, desperate, unable to help himself. There is no mention of faith. He is not asked if he believes and there is no hint that he became a disciple of Jesus. In fact, he does not even ask Jesus' name and simply did not know who had healed him. After Jesus sought him out, he was quizzed by Jewish officials and did not hesitate to tell the Jews who it was that had healed him. As Leon Morris observed, this man was 'not of the stuff of which heroes are made'.[5]

Such a poor and helpless man is a reminder that this is how it is with all of us. He was picked out of the crowd and was chosen by Jesus, just as believers today have no merit but are chosen by Jesus. For him it had been thirty-eight years of misery and then this! We too have no claims on God. Grace is always undeserved.

Doesn't it strike you as rather odd that Jesus asked him: 'Do you want to be made well?' (5:6). This was not a test or tricky question. Jesus wished to engage with the poor man. His question points to a possibility; it whispers an invitation. Do you really want an altogether different life? You will never be the same again. Do you really want to be changed?

As we hear this dialogue, we too are confronted with the reminder that the Great Healer comes to us right where we are and speaks to us just as we are. 'Do you want change? Do you want me to upend all your values and ways of being? Do you want to be made well?'

Of course we recognise that for some sad people the question has a startling relevance. Some people 'enjoy' poor health. Hypochondriacs are sometimes amusing if tragic figures, anxious to avoid the responsibilities of good health. They both want and do not want to be made whole. Perhaps we too fear the cure more than the illness, prefer the familiarity of our old life rather than risk the inevitable change if we follow Jesus? As William Temple suggested: 'It is part of the deadly quality of sin that it hinders us from seeking its cure'.[6]

'Do you want to be made whole again?' We are told that the man in response did not assert 'Of course!' but rather rehearsed the obstacles to his being cured. He was too lame to get there first and had no one who would help him. Perhaps he hoped that Jesus was a potential friend, but who knew how long it might be before the waters were stirred again (possibly caused by a bubbling from a spring)? 'Left to himself, locked in defeat and incapacity, he can see no further. He is not yet aware of any divine possibilities in the situation.'[7]

Jesus did not need an imaginary angel to stir the waters. He simply commanded the man: 'Stand up! Take your mat! Walk!' Three brief commands and the man showed a measure of trust in this stranger by doing exactly what he was told to do. At once he was healed and off he went—naturally a bit wobbly—carrying his simple mat, probably woven from palm leaves. Once again, hearing the word of Jesus brought dramatic change.

John Calvin made a sensitive observation about what happened. 'We keep our attention fixed on the means which are within our reach, and … contrary to expectation, [God] displays his hand from hidden places, and thus shows how far his goodness goes beyond the narrow limits of our faith'.[8]

That is not the end of this story of course. But we must pause to emphasise that this is truly a parable of grace. He is a man who had absolutely no claim on Jesus. There is no evidence that he was an immoral or even especially moral person. He is simply a receiver. FB Craddock asks: 'Can grace be more radically presented? Even those of us who think we believe in grace are by this story stripped of everything'.[9] We too easily begin to think that our faith is a kind of good work drawing down God's favour on us.

Moreover, the traditions surrounding this pool suggested the possibility of a healing that only favoured the strong. The weak were always left out. Some of our churches can be similar. We seem to be a place that offers a new beginning but all too often the 'unsuitable' and most crippled do not find a welcome. This story of an invalid being cured reminds us that the life Jesus chooses to give (see 5:21) is not only for those who seem to be deserving—people 'like us'. This is how Jesus found us all, incorrigible and claimless, debilitated by our sickness and our failures. That is how Paul described his church at Corinth: 'not wise by human standards, not powerful, not of noble birth … the low and despised in the world'

(1 Cor. 1:26). This lame man would have fitted into the church at Corinth. Would he be so easily welcomed into our comfortable churches?

The invitation comes to us so that we can cease being a victim of circumstances and of life's cruel impact. The question for us is: are we willing to receive the gift of grace and then stand on our own two feet and accept responsibility for those cripples who still lie beside the pool of false hope? No more isolation living in a hell of dis-ease. Instead we are reconnected to God's world and the family of humanity! One of the symbols of salvation found in the ancient catacomb paintings was of a man rising from baptismal waters carrying a bed upon his back.

So it is that our deliverance is entirely an undeserved act of grace. Robert Capon, in *Between Noon and Three: Romance, Law and the Outrage of Grace* (1997), raises deep understandings about forgiveness and grace. The hours between noon and three, of course, are the hours that Jesus hung on the cross. Among many striking passages is this:

> The life of grace is not an effort on our part to achieve a goal we set ourselves. It is a continually renewed attempt simply to believe that someone else has done all the achieving that is needed, and to live in relationship with that person, whether we achieve it or not. If that doesn't seem like much to you, you're right: it isn't. And as a matter of fact, the life of grace is even less than that. It's not even our life at all, but the life of that Someone Else rising like a tide in the ruins of our death.[10]

HEALING ON THE SABBATH IS A SIGN THAT JESUS IS THE SON OF GOD (5:10–18)

We are told: 'Now that day was a sabbath' (5:9). Why did Jesus heal on that day? Some naturally ask: 'Well why not?' As Calvin remarked: 'Why wait?' At a festival there were crowds, so many more could be challenged by the miracle. It is never the wrong day to do the will of God. But Jesus slipped away from the crowds; publicity does not seem to have been on his mind.

That it was a sabbath led to the controversy. Hostile critics surrounded the poor man, recovering from his decades-long suffering. The Jewish rabbis had developed some thirty-nine classifications of what constituted 'work' and all were forbidden by this commandment. They debated, for example, whether or not it was permissible to 'carry' artificial teeth or a wooden leg.[11] The man in John's account had to live in a world where people did not like the unexpected—certainly not something which challenged their traditional ways.

The obsession of the religious leaders meant that they ignored the miracle but pounced on this poor man for carrying his mat on a sabbath. By a convoluted and bizarre reasoning, carrying one's mat was counted as bearing a burden on the sabbath. 'The Jews' focused on the challenge of the conventional order, whereas Jesus and the healed man focused on the possibilities of a new life. As Schnackenburg analysed the situation: 'The one acting with the authority of God comes into conflict with the human custodians and exponents of God's law'.[12]

We should be clear that Jesus understood and respected the institution of the sabbath. He does not abrogate or contradict sabbath law. The sabbath was written into the order of creation and Jesus does not challenge or change that order. The value and truth of the sabbath as a principle of living is being rediscovered again in our generation, when many tired and overworked people find renewal and relief in a freely-observed wisdom of rest. God still urges a regular sabbath break.

But God's work does not stop on the sabbath or any other day. As Lesslie Newbigin explains: 'It seems to have been accepted by the rabbis that God's Sabbath rest did not mean that he had ceased to give life—for babies are born on the Sabbath and rain falls … God is always—even on the Sabbath—the giver of life'.[13]

That is the exact point that Jesus made on that sabbath in Jerusalem. 'Whatever the Father does, the Son does likewise' (5:19). Jesus is one with the Father. His work is identical to the Father's. Equality with God is what Jesus claimed, and that is precisely why the Jews began to plot his death. How dare he make himself equal with God (5:18)!

The astonishing fact is that they did not seem to be interested in how the man had been healed. The same thing happened when the religious leaders examined a man who had been healed of his blindness (9:1–41). Rather, the experts were only interested in how this strange healer could really be a good man if he did not obey their rules and regulations.

The recovered paralytic eventually was found by Jesus and the cure was followed by another word. He was charged not to sin any more or something worse would happen to him (5:14). 'The power of Jesus to give life and his authority to forgive sins are inseparable.'[14] This does not mean that his illness was the result of some earlier sin, an idea which Jesus explicitly rejects in a later miracle (9:3). Rather, the man was called to live a changed and responsible life, in obedience to the one who had cured him. The sin which he was here warned against was unbelief; and, as he does not appear to have become a disciple of Jesus, the warning of ultimate judgement was urgent and final.

The message of this chapter is that Jesus is obedient to the Father's will and work. 'My father is still working [on the sabbath, as on every day] and I also am working' (5:17). Jesus is doing God's work. That work is not the kind of occupation that Jewish laws forbade on the sabbath. He is restoring life. He has come to bring life, and he has come that all his followers might have that life abundantly (10:10). The claim is that he is doing God's work—giving life—because he is God's Son. In the ancient world a person's agent is as himself. Jesus in this sense is the agent of his Father. Like Father, like Son. Jesus cannot *not* heal on the sabbath, or on any other day.

The long conversation between Jesus and the Jews (5:19–47) stresses who Jesus is. The miracle showed what Jesus does: he brings grace, hope and healing to needy souls. The fact that he did it on a sabbath enables him to teach who he is—one with the Father, the Son of God.

CS Lewis made a powerful and oft-cited defence of the claims of Jesus to be the Son of God:

> In the mouth of any speaker who is not God, these words would imply what I can only regard as silliness and conceit unrivalled by any character in history … You must make your choice. Either this man was, and is, the Son of God; or else a madman or something worse. You can shut him up for a fool, you can spit at him and kill him as a demon; or you can fall at his feet and call him Lord and God.[15]

Thornton Wilder wrote a simple but powerful short play based on this story in John 5, *The Angel that troubled the Waters* (1928*)*. Wilder gives the story a surprising twist. He adapts the story: whoever gets into the water first, after the angel stirs it, is healed. But a physician who suffers with 'festering limbs, with my heart in pain' has been waiting for years for his chance. He is there when the waters are stirred and rushes to seize his chance of healing. But the angel appears to him before he can enter the pool, stops him and says:

> Without your wound where would your power be? It is your very sadness that makes your low voice tremble into the hearts of men. The very angels themselves cannot persuade the wretched and blundering children on earth as can one human being broken on the wheels of living. In Love's service only the wounded soldiers can serve. Draw back.

Later, the person who does enter the pool and is healed rejoices in this blessing but then turns to the physician and says:

> But come with me first, an hour only, to my home. My son is lost in dark thoughts and only you have ever lifted his mood. Only an hour … my daughter since her child has died, sits in the shadow. She will not listen to us …[16]

This play is a powerful reminder of what Paul later discovered: that he could only boast of his wounds and weaknesses and that God's grace was sufficient, that his power was made perfect in weakness (2 Cor. 12:9). 'Without your wound where would your power be?' This is a profound encouragement to many believers who question why no angel, nor even Jesus himself, has come to heal them. Our wounds can offer a compassion and understanding that the healthy and comfortable cannot bring: 'only the wounded soldiers can serve'.

There are, then, several aspects of truth found in this miracle-sign. Above all, the story calls us to join in wonder with the disciple who confessed to the one whose wounds he had wished to see and touch: 'My Lord and my God' (20:28).

Questions for discussion

1. 'Google' the pool of Bethesda and study the ruins and the accounts of the pool. Can you imagine Jesus and the man there? What might be a modern parallel to this pool?

2. Why do you think Jesus asked the man if he wanted to be healed? Discuss the quotation from William Temple: 'It is part of the deadly quality of sin that it hinders us from seeking its cure'.

3. In what sense is this story a powerful parable of undeserved grace?

4. Discuss the quotation from Capon about the 'outrage of grace'.

5. We marvel at the legalism of the Jews in the time of Jesus. Can you identify any ways in which modern believers slip into a kind of legalism about the way Christians should live?

6. Explore the argument of CS Lewis that Jesus was either mad or truly the Son of God.

7. Can you summarise what this reading tells us about Jesus? Think about how this is relevant for us today.

8. 'Without your wound where would your power be?' Can you think of situations where this line from Wilder would be helpful?

1. CS Keener, *The Gospel of John. A Commentary* (Peabody Mass.: Hendrickson, 2003), p. 636.

2. GD Fee, 'On the Inauthenticity of John 5:3b–4', *Evangelical Quarterly* 54 (1982), 218.

3. G Theissen, as cited by Keener, *The Gospel of John*, p. 638.

4. For the use of *Cocoon* see PD Duke, 'John 5:1–18', *Review and Expositor* 88 (1988), 539.

5. L Morris, *The Gospel According to John* (Grand Rapids: Eerdmans, 1995), p. 306.

6. W Temple, *Readings in St John's Gospel* (London: Macmillan, 1961[1939–40]), p. 105.

7. AJ Kelly and FJ Moloney, *Experiencing God in the Gospel of John* (New York: Paulist Press, 2003), p. 116.

8. J Calvin, as cited by K Pidcock-Lester, 'John 5:1–9', *Interpretation*, 59 (2005), 61.

9. FB Craddock, *John* (Atlanta: John Knox Press, 1982), p. 44.

10. RF Capon, *Between Noon and Three: Romance, Law and the Outrage of Grace* (Grand Rapids: Eerdmans, 1997).

11. W Barclay, *The Gospel of John* (Daily Study Bible; Edinburgh: Saint Andrew Press, 1955), vol 1, p. 178.

12. R Shnackenburg, as cited by F Moloney, *The Gospel of John* (Collegeville, Minn.: Liturgical Press, 1998), p. 171.

13. L Newbigin, *The Light Has Come: An Exposition of the Fourth Gospel* (Grand Rapids: Eerdmans, 1982), p. 65.

14. A Schlatter, as cited by EC Hoskyns, *The Fourth Gospel* (London: Faber and Faber, 1947), p. 266.

15. CS Lewis, *Mere Christianity* (New York: Macmillan 1952), p. 55.

16. T Wilder, *The Angel that Troubled the Waters* www.9th-hour.ca/wp-content/uploads/.../The-Angel-That-Troubled-the-Waters.pdf, accessed 27/9/16.

'The Miracle of the Loaves and Fishes', Lambert Lombard, c. 1550

CHAPTER FIVE

IMAGINE ALL THE PEOPLE: JESUS AND THE HUNGRY CROWD
(JOHN 6:1–15)

To be confronted by an overwhelming problem is always a huge challenge. Problems come in various forms but there is something especially challenging when the problem takes the form of human need. So, when we read about Jesus facing an excited and hungry crowd of some 5,000 with scarcely anything to offer them for food, we can begin to imagine how the disciples felt. Jesus actually placed Philip under the spotlight: 'Where are we to buy bread for these people to eat?' (John 6:5).

This strangely modern question still haunts humankind. Despite the good life which so many of us enjoy in the developed world, humanity today faces overwhelming problems of need. 'All these people' are refugees fleeing from war-torn Syria and other tragic situations. Millions are starving even though the world has more than sufficient resources to feed every man, woman and child. 'Where can we buy places of refuge or food for all these people?' We cannot help thinking about these twenty-first century problems as we read of this miraculous feeding of the 5,000. This story is told in all four gospels, which suggests its importance for the earliest believers, although we need to look closely at how John weaves his theology into his version. Can what happened back then on that grassy hilltop help us today?

A popular song by John Lennon captured the deep sense of injustice in the world, and a longing for a new way of living: imagine a world without possessions, greed or hunger; imagine the world being shared equally by all. This chapter invites us to reflect on these most fundamental human issues. Is there any link between the teachings of Jesus and the utopian dream of the Beatles?

Central to the story is that Jesus was able to take a tiny gift, 'five barley loaves and two fish' to be precise, and then feed a multitude. Naturally the story has inspired successive generations to imagine what God might do with seemingly inadequate and even ludicrous offerings.

How might this story and the long passage of Jesus' teaching which follows (6:25–65) help us face the seemingly impossible tasks we face?

ALL THESE PEOPLE: A PROBLEM AND A TEST (JOHN 6:1–15)

Once again this story is specifically designated a 'sign' (6:14), so we are alerted that we need to look beyond the externals of what Jesus did to what it reveals about him. Jesus had travelled across the Sea of Galilee (later named 'Tiberias' after the emperor). Jesus adopted the position of teacher on the mountain and in classic rabbinical manner sat down with his disciples. John adds that it was the time of Passover (6:4); this would explain why it was that time of the year when there was a lush growth of grass, but, more significantly, places the whole chapter in the context of the Passover and the sacrifice that Jesus will make. Passover meant that deliverance and freedom from bondage were all the talk amongst Jewish people. There may also be a link with the experiences of Israel in the wilderness at the time that God 'rained down manna upon them to eat, and gave them the grain of heaven' (Psalm 78:24).

A large crowd had swarmed after Jesus. They 'followed' him (6:2) but not in the sense of those who became new disciples; rather, they followed him because they had seen the 'signs' he had performed in healing the sick. So the seemingly impossible problem emerged. How could this large number of people be fed?

We are told that the question to Philip—'Where are we to buy bread for these people to eat?'—constituted a kind of test. John, who always depicts Jesus as in control of events, adds that Jesus asked this because 'he knew what he was going to do'. In what sense was this a test for Philip? Presumably, it was to test his faith in advance of any miracle. By this incident Jesus tested all his disciples' faith in order to prepare them for the larger tests to come (see 6:67–71). The response of Philip was that of a bookkeeper who had calculated the cash that would have been needed, even if there had been any supermarkets out there in that remote place! He simply stressed the literal impossibility of buying anything like what would be needed (6:7).

At this point Andrew, who was always on the lookout for people to bring to Jesus (1:40), brought a boy with his meagre lunch of five barley loaves (or buns, as we might say, the bread of the very poor), and two pickled fish (probably about the size of sardines). He was not necessarily a very young child as the word used here could be used of someone as old as 17. But Andrew's wistful comment haunts us: 'But what are these among so many people?'

In John's version, however, notice that Jesus is in complete control. He tells his friends to organise the people to sit down and after giving thanks he personally distributed the food (6:10–11) whereas the other gospels indicate that the disciples gave out the food. How many Sunday school teachers have embellished this story, imagining the boy's mother lovingly preparing this small lunch pack and urging him to be careful with it! How the boy came to tell Andrew about it is unknown, but clearly the unnamed boy was willing to share what little he had that others might have something. This naturally is a spiritual lesson that has often been drawn by preachers and is an important principle of Christian service.

All four gospels quite clearly depict the feeding as a miracle. A rationalistic age looks to find an alternative explanation. Barclay, for example, introduces 'another and very lovely explanation'. He suggests that the example of the boy prompted others to share what they had—and it seems unlikely that people would have set off on a walk of over nine miles without any provisions. True, the text does not actually say that this was the only food available, but that is not the point. The miracle, according to this interpretation, is that in the presence of Jesus a crowd of selfish men and women became 'a fellowship of sharers'.[1]

But as William Temple observed: 'If the Lord was indeed God incarnate, the story presents no insuperable difficulties'.[2] If we believe in the incarnation—that 'the word became flesh', as John put it (1:14)—then this and all the other miracles of Jesus become a matter of reasonable and responsible faith. Moreover, there were twelve baskets of food left over, a symbol of the abundance of provision that Jesus makes for the needy (see 10:10).

We are not told exactly how it happened. Whether people in the crowd understood the full extent of what was happening is uncertain, but the important fact is that they perceived that this was a 'sign' and their conclusion was that Jesus was indeed 'the prophet who is to come into the world' (6:14). This is most probably an allusion to the 'prophet like Moses' (Deuteronomy 18:18) who would once again bring down manna from heaven. As Jewish tradition saw Moses as a king, the determination of the crowd to make Jesus a king (6:15) is understandable. At long last—they would have hoped—they would be led out of the oppression that the Romans had imposed upon them.

Adopting Jesus as a kind of political hero is to misunderstand his identity and mission. This is not faith but unbelief. As Lesslie Newbigin has observed:

> They have not understood who Jesus is. Jesus will not be the instrument of any human enthusiasm or the symbol for any human program. To say 'Jesus is King' is true if the word 'king' is wholly defined by the person of Jesus; it is false and blasphemous if

> Jesus is made instrumental to a definition of kingship derived from elsewhere. Jesus has come to 'proclaim liberty to the captives' but he will not become the mascot for a people's movement of liberation.[3]

In other words, what Lennon imagined in his song as a brave new brotherhood is only possible if Jesus is recognised as our true King, and under his rule lies the only hope of any ultimate sharing of life and possessions.

What we should learn from this problem and this test, as recorded in John 6, is that we can always trust Jesus to provide what is needed, however great the challenge. Our faith and our willingness to offer what we have is the crucial matter. Even the church is regularly tested as to whether we truly rely on Jesus or try to gain what we seek by a religious–political alignment. This is always unbelief. This is not to reject the need for Christian protest against injustice and the necessity to work for human need, but it is to insist that the focus of our hope is in the kingdom of God, not political alliances.

This does not, of course, diminish our Christian responsibility to do all we can to assist those who are hungry or in great need. Together, through World Vision and through our various denominational agencies, we must seek (in numerous ways) to offer this compassionate action.

Australian Baptists in particular should recall how this story inspired the pioneer missionaries sent out on their behalf. In 1885, Silas Mead of the Flinders Street Baptist Church in Adelaide—the leading figure in challenging his denomination to share in world mission—based his farewell address on this story. Before him were five young women—Ellen Arnold, Martha Plested, Marion Fuller, Ruth Wilkin and Alice Pappin—who were preparing to serve among the millions of Bengalis in India. He recalled the 'five barley loaves' and asked: 'What were they among so many people?' How could five women possibly have an impact on millions of Bengali women? These five women acquired an iconic status as the 'Five Barley Loaves' who began the 'foreign' (cross-cultural) mission work of Australian Baptists.[4] A 'multitude' of believers have flowed from the work that began with such a tiny and inexperienced group.

FEEDING ALL THESE PEOPLE: A SIGN THAT JESUS IS THE BREAD OF LIFE

We need to be very clear that John did not place this story here simply to affirm Jesus as a wonder-worker. The 'sign' was pointing to the reality of Jesus as the Son of God. This is made very clear in the dialogue which follows later in the chapter. Jesus removed himself from the temptation to be made a king (6:15). We recall the temptations as described in Luke, where Jesus was invited to receive all glory and authority from the kingdoms of the world (Luke 4:5–8). Here, once again, he resisted that particular temptation and withdrew to the mountain. Later, after yet another miracle (as the disciples were caught in a fierce storm on the lake), he again taught the crowd of pilgrims.

In this dialogue (6:25–65) Jesus drew out the deep meaning of the feeding of the crowd. He urged them not to be satisfied with the food that perishes but with what he called 'the food that endures for eternal life' (6:27). This is to be linked with what Jesus had told the woman of Samaria when he spoke to her about life-giving water. These two fundamental and universal symbols of the sources of life are declared to be found—in a deep spiritual sense—in Jesus. He later insists: 'I am the bread of life. Those who come to me will never be hungry; those who believe in me will never be thirsty' (6:35); 'I am the living bread that comes down from heaven. If anyone eats this bread he will live forever' (6:51). John repeatedly reports that Jesus said: 'I am …' and these loved 'I am' sayings of Jesus illuminate his meaning for believers.

Jesus knew that there are two kinds of hunger: physical hunger (which physical food can satisfy) and spiritual hunger (which only Jesus can satisfy). Many today manifest this spiritual hunger in diverse ways. In the quest for fulfilment some turn to various drugs, or pursue their careers with manic determination, but they find that these addictions never give the satisfaction they are seeking. Philosophers and seekers have often acknowledged the hunger for purpose and fulfilment, which, Christians argue, can only be found in Jesus as the bread of life.

What is made clear in the midst of this expressive metaphor about Jesus is that 'feeding on him' is the act of believing. There is the most graphic development of this in the words of Jesus about 'eating his flesh and drinking his blood' (6:53–68). This is reminiscent of the eucharist, when believers eat and drink bread and wine and so 'feed' on Christ. This kind of language caused grave misunderstandings for some in the early church. Some outsiders heard garbled accounts of what Christians did when they gathered for worship, and this talk of eating flesh and drinking blood led them to accuse believers of cannibalism!

Scholars disagree over the extent to which John in this chapter is teaching about the eucharist. It is not necessary to understand these verses in this way, but it remains a challenging understanding of who Jesus is and what believing in him means. Bruce Milne offers a convincing comment:

> The eating of his flesh and the drinking of his blood would appear a vivid, even shocking, illustration of what 'believing' in him implies. In its earthiness, however, the image is ideally suited to the materialistic mindset of his audience ... Interpreting the passage in this way, however, does not preclude our recognizing that Jesus' imagery came to life in a new way in the later experience of the church as it shared the meal Jesus initiated.[5]

The miracle and the teaching together challenge us about whether we truly believe in Jesus in this comprehensive way. Do we find in Jesus alone our very life, our nourishment, and our purpose? Only in this way, insists Jesus himself, can we find eternal life.

Indeed, the final scene of the chapter raises a striking question for each one of us. John records that many of the Jews were deeply offended by what Jesus had said and the disciples themselves blurted out that this was a very difficult kind of talk (6:52, 60). Jesus confronted them and reminded them that there was an inescapable and exclusive claim which they had to face. 'My words are spirit and life. But among you there are some who do not believe' (6:63–64). Even today some still hope to find—through church involvement, for example—the valuable business contacts that they need to advance their cause. Self-serving has no place amongst those who claim to be followers of Jesus.

After the challenging words of Jesus, many of his would-be disciples turned away and no longer 'went about with him'. Jesus must have been disappointed by this shallow response and turned to his inner circle, the twelve, and asked them face to face: 'Do you also wish to go away?' (6:66–67). Simon Peter, always the impetuous spokesman, confessed: 'Lord, to whom can we go? You have the words of eternal life. We have come to believe and know that you are the Holy One of God' (6:68–69).

Unbelief cannot remain hidden. There is always a testing as to the reality of our faith. Even among the twelve there was one who would become an apostate. Even though Jesus had chosen them he was forced to lament: 'One of you is a devil' (6:70). The story of Judas is the theme of a later chapter, but already the reader is alerted to the fact that Jesus is not taken by surprise as he is the one who knows what is in each person.

What John here stresses is that within those who seek to follow Jesus there are both those who will remain and those who will leave him. Belief and unbelief are both present and both are individual choices. Yet both belief and unbelief remained within the first company of those whom he had chosen. Jesus had called them all, but they remained free—free to be with him or leave him.

This rather salutary reminder poses a question for each of us. To believe is to trust Jesus absolutely; no one else can decide for us, just as no one else is responsible for how we respond to the call of Jesus. Is it perhaps time for each of us to renew our response to Jesus, and to affirm that only in him do we find our life and our sustenance?

Where are you and I in this story? Am I the boy who generously shares what he has? Are we among those who have been fed? We are not told about what effect eating there on that day had on those who received these unexpected gifts from Jesus. It must have been a time of hilarity and sharing, a picnic lying on the grass and eating their full. Did they tell the story over and over again, and did some of them follow Jesus? Or am I like the majority of the enthusiastic crowd, who wanted leaders who would not only give them bread and water but would feed their greed? Or are we like the disciples who confessed: 'To whom else can we go?'

Questions for discussion

1. Can you imagine how this story could encourage you as you face a major problem?

2. How might a Christian believer respond to John Lennon's song *Imagine all the people*? In what ways could we share that vision and in what ways might a Christian want to address the problems of world hunger?

3. In what ways was the question of Jesus to Philip a test (6:8)? If you had been Philip how would you have responded to what Jesus said and did?

4. Explore the relevance of this story, especially Jesus' refusal to be crowned a king by the crowd, to the question of how Christians should seek to bring about change in the world. Do you think some groups do try to make Jesus a kind of 'mascot' to their cause?

5. How do you understand the teaching that as believers we are to feed on the flesh of Jesus and drink his blood? Can you relate this to sharing in the communion service?

6. What exactly does it mean to you to think of Jesus as the Bread of Life?

1. W Barclay, *The Gospel of John* (Edinburgh: Saint Andrew Press, 1955), Vol. 1, p. 206.

2. W Temple, *Readings in St John's Gospel* (London: Macmillan, 1961), p. 74.

3. L Newbigin, *The Light has come. An Exposition of the Fourth Gospel* (Grand Rapids: Eerdmans, 1982) p. 76.

4. See T Cupit, R Gooden and K Manley (eds), *From Five Barley Loaves. Australian Baptists in Global Mission 1864–2010* (Preston, Vic: Mosaic Press, 2013).

5. B Milne, *The Message of John: Here is your King!* (Downers Grove, Ill.: InterVarsity Press, 1993), p. 113.

'Christ Preaching at Capernaum', Maurycy Gottlieb, 1879

CHAPTER SIX

COME OUT IN THE OPEN: JESUS AND HIS BROTHERS
(JOHN 7:1–13)

The challenge to 'come out in the open', as *The Message* translates John 7:4, has a modern ring to it. There were no secrets to be uncovered about Jesus. But the taunt—for such it seems to have been—opens up a wide range of issues relating to Jesus, his family and his mission.

For readers of John this encounter between Jesus and his family bristles with questions and challenges. There are questions about the family of Jesus which have always intrigued people—how did Jesus relate to his earthly family? Some of us struggle to establish our own identities when parents or siblings stifle us, mock us or engage in personal criticisms of us. For many of us, on the other hand, the love and support of our family is unbelievably assuring. The relative silence of the Bible about the family of Jesus has spawned, from the earliest days to modern times, fanciful and often objectionable fantasies about this special family. Long-kept secrets are alleged to surround Jesus and his family and the hysterical 'uncovering' of such bizarre possibilities has fascinated some modern novelists and filmmakers.[1]

The challenge of the story is in the questions it poses. What exactly was the meaning of this dialogue between Jesus and his brothers? Why did Jesus say he was not going to a major Jewish festival with his brothers, and then some time later travel privately to that event? Is there theological and spiritual significance in this encounter and its aftermath? How does any of this help a modern disciple of Jesus?

JESUS, HIS BROTHERS AND A JEWISH FESTIVAL

As is always necessary, our first task is to look closely at how John introduces this verbal exchange between Jesus and his brothers. Chapters 7 to 12 record what Westcott called 'the great controversy' in which faith and unbelief are revealed.[2] Within this larger section, Chapters 7 and 8 form a unity marked by the notes of secrecy in 7:4 and 8:59.

The previous chapter had concluded with many of the disciples in Judea leaving Jesus and here we are told that Jesus was back in Galilee and 'walked about', which tells us how he itinerated, sharing his message. That he did not wish to return to Judea is understandable since 'the Jews' wished to find opportunity to kill him (7:1).

Six months after the Passover, which was the setting of Chapter 6, another major Jewish festival was to take place in Jerusalem. The feast of tabernacles (or booths) was one of the most sacred of Jewish festivals and was regarded as among the most popular and joyous. This is the setting for these next chapters, and an understanding of what took place will help us understand many aspects of Jesus' actions and words. This feast included elements of an earlier form of harvest festival: temporary outdoor shelters ('booths' or 'tabernacles') were erected and God's gifts of water and rain were celebrated. The flimsy tents evoked the memory of the tents when Israel wandered in the desert. Goodspeed paraphrased it as 'the Jewish camping festival'[3], although, as one (undoubtedly English) commentator observed, it shared 'both the discomfort and merriment of a picnic'.[4] The men celebrating the festival slept and ate meals in the booths for the seven days of the festival, after which (on the eighth day) there was a special feast.

According to later Jewish writings, within this festival there were three major elements. The first was the water libation ceremony, when priests and Levites went daily to the pool of Siloam (which features in Chapter 9) and gathered water which was taken to the temple altar and poured out. This was the context in which Jesus spoke about the 'rivers of living water', the Holy Spirit that Jesus promised his followers (7:37–39). The second feature of the feast was the ceremony of light when four menorahs were set up in the centre of the court of the women; this was the background to the claim of Jesus that he was 'the light of the world' (8:12). The final rite was 'facing the temple', when at sunrise the priests would turn their backs on the sun and face the sanctuary of the Temple.

Every Jewish male had the duty to travel to this 'pilgrim feast', so it was not surprising that the brothers of Jesus were determined to be there. They asked Jesus to go from Galilee to Judea (not specifically for this feast) arguing that if he did this the works of Jesus might be seen by 'your disciples' (7:3). This is where they urged him: 'Come out into the open'. They reasoned that no one who wants to be widely known acts in secret. 'A revelation is no revelation at all if it is not revealed.'[5]

Then a significant comment was added: '*If* you do these things …' This was a shrewd and presumably insulting condition. They misunderstood the purpose of the 'signs' or 'works' that Jesus had done. John adds the frank comment that 'not even his brothers believed in him' (7:5). Incidentally, that this verse is included indicates that the writer was not trying to ignore any embarrassing facts; it is here in all its unvarnished frankness.

The reply of Jesus is revealing: 'My time has not yet come' (7:6). The word used for time here is not 'hour' as is so frequent in John; instead (in the only instance in the gospel) he refers to his *kairos*. This word suggests the 'best' time, a unique opportunity. Yet this moment was not the time that God had determined for

Jesus to act in this way. On the other hand, because the brothers were still part of the 'world', any time suited them. They could go in safety and freedom, for the 'world'—that is, humankind in opposition to God—would not seek them nor wish to destroy them. In contrast, Jesus insisted he was not going to the festival because his *kairos* had not yet fully come. Readers of the gospel know that his destiny—his *kairos*—is to be the encounter in Jerusalem when he is lifted up on the cross.

There are two questions to be considered. First, who exactly were his 'brothers'? Roman Catholics and others committed to a belief in the perpetual virginity of Mary deny that these were her children. Some suggest that they were children of Joseph from a previous marriage (for which there is no evidence) and others suggest that 'brothers' here actually means 'cousins'. Again, this is highly unlikely. The gospels speak of four men as brothers of Jesus: James, Joses (or Joseph), Simon and Judas (or Jude). See Matthew 13:55, which also refers to his sisters. Jesus was the firstborn, which makes the mocking of his siblings quite disconcerting since in Jewish tradition honouring kinship was very important, especially honouring the eldest in a family. The only previous reference to the family in John is in the story of the wedding feast at Cana, where Mary and the brothers were present but there is no mention of them believing in Jesus after that miracle (2:12).

There are a few other significant references to the family in the New Testament. One of the most surprising is the fact that his mother and brothers at one point sought to restrain him and thought he had gone mad! (Mark 3:21, 31–34 // Matthew 12:46–50). It is striking that on the cross Jesus commended his mother to his disciple John and not to a family member (19:26–27). However, Mary and the brothers were in Jerusalem after the ascension of Jesus (Acts 1:14). Afterwards, some of his brothers were active in the church, notably James who became the leader in Jerusalem (1 Corinthians 9:5; 15:7; Acts 12:17; 15:13; 21:18; Galatians 1:19; 2: 29; James 1:1). By tradition, Jude was the author of his letter (Jude 1). Clearly the resurrection of Jesus had been decisive in moving the brothers from unbelief to faith.

But what are we to make of this ironic saying of the brothers? 'Come out into the open if you are the real thing!' If you really want to recruit more followers, head to where the action is, where the crowds are gathered. This was sound political advice.

What is somewhat disconcerting is the fact that after the brothers had gone on their pilgrimage Jesus then proceeded to go to Jerusalem! He did this in secret (7:10). How could he do that? Did he lie to his brothers? That this was a problem for early readers is suggested by the fact that some manuscripts have Jesus saying to the brothers: 'I am *not yet* going'. Surely the simple explanation is that the writer is emphasising that Jesus acts only when the Father indicates to him that this is what must be done. Jesus did not allow his mother at the wedding in Cana to determine his action but he later proceeded to help her. Again, with the officer whose son was sick, Jesus appeared to do nothing at first; and in the raising of Lazarus there was also a delay before Jesus went to the grieving family. He was not going with his brothers when they wanted him to go, but went when his *kairos* had come.

Craddock suggests that this story, in which Jesus' own brothers found it so hard to accept his claims and to believe in him, is another reminder that even those who lived at the same time and were in the closest proximity to Jesus found it hard to believe. They had no absolute advantage over those of us who, centuries later, have only the word and witness of his followers to prompt our faith. Those closest to him did not have any advantage: 'Even members of Jesus' own family did not believe in him'.[6] That austere reformer Calvin observed: 'The children of God suffer worse annoyance from their relations than from outsiders, for [their relations] are Satan's instruments to tempt either to ambition or to avarice those who desired to serve God purely and faithfully'.[7] Morris adds: 'Many a man faced with cruel opposition in public life has been sustained by the faith and the faithfulness of his kith and kin. Jesus was denied this solace'.[8]

There are, I suggest, two other reflections for a modern reader. The first is the importance of waiting for God's time in all our activities. How easily we can rush into ventures of witness or other service without a careful waiting on God prior to the task. This is not an excuse for delay in beginning some mission but recognises the importance of timing as important for us too. The example of Jesus in ignoring the urging of non-believers to act in a certain way is relevant.

This story is also an example of not being diverted from a special call by family reservations or opposition. William Carey, the pioneer of the modern missionary movement, was so convinced of his duty to take the gospel to India that he was prepared to travel without his wife Dorothy, who was naturally hesitant to undertake such a journey from her English village to an unknown world. In the event, a shipping delay meant that Carey was able to make a quick trip home and Dorothy agreed to come if her sister accompanied her. Carey was willing to respond to what he believed to be the call of God and even family opposition did not dissuade him. This was an unusual and extreme example of not allowing family to dissuade one from a call of God, and no mission society would allow it today! Dorothy endured great physical and mental anguish for much of her time in India, although Carey never wavered from his calling and became a great missionary leader.[9]

In lesser ways we may face determined ridicule and even opposition from family members. We should ensure that we do not unnecessarily provoke, aggravate nor intensify family tensions, but if this is our situation then this story of the courage and faithfulness of Jesus when faced with family opposition can inspire and strengthen us.

JESUS AT THE FESTIVAL: QUESTIONS AND OPPOSITION

Jerusalem had become a dangerous place for Jesus. He acted secretly until the middle of the feast when the largest crowds were present. He was able to blend into the crowds, reminding us that there was nothing supernatural or strange in his appearance—he 'became flesh and lived among us' (1:14). The word here is 'tabernacled' among us, a reminder perhaps of this feast. As Keener summarises: 'Probably he looked like most of his Palestinian Jewish contemporaries, wearing a beard; more likely than not he had a light brown complexion with black hair'.[10]

The crowd was divided (7:12) and the Judaism of this period was quite diverse on several issues. Those at this feast would have come from all over the Jewish world. Westcott claimed that no section of the gospel is 'more evidently a transcript from life than this. It reflects a complex and animated variety of characters and feelings'.[11] People with widely different hopes and questions are presented. Some in the crowd rejected Jesus; others affirmed that he was 'a good man'. It is important to recall that although John consistently depicts 'the Jews' as condemning Jesus, at the same time Jesus was himself a Jew and many other Jews followed him. Here we have Jewish people at a Jewish festival not daring to speak about Jesus because of 'fear of the Jews'! The uninformed majority are not necessarily what John means by the 'Jews'. As a later chapter will discuss, opposition by the 'Jews' is by a particular group of leaders and not the whole community.

Brown suggests that the three requests made of Jesus in Chapters 6 and 7 correspond to the three temptations which Jesus faced in the wilderness (see Matthew 4:1–11 and Luke 4:1–13):[12] (1) the people wished to make him king (6:15) and Satan offered him the kingdoms of the world; (2) the people asked for miraculous bread (6:31) and Satan invited Jesus to turn the stones into bread; (3) the brothers wanted Jesus to go to Jerusalem and show his power (7:3) and Satan took Jesus to the temple and invited him to display his power by jumping from the pinnacle. Thus the dramatic presentations of the temptations in the desert were probably temptations that Jesus faced in a more prosaic way throughout his ministry. Satan did not give up easily.

The whole chapter repays careful analysis and reflection. John tells us that for the first time Jesus went to the temple to teach (7:14) and this very deed provoked great astonishment among his hearers. How dare this man teach in such an authoritative and independent way! Does he link himself with Moses? By what authority?

The reply of Jesus states a major theme of the gospel—Jesus and his teaching are sent directly from God the Father. He asserts how hearers may interpret the meaning of his words: 'If you do the will of God you will know whether the teaching is from God or on my own authority' (7:17). Jesus is not speaking from any motive of self-promotion: 'there is nothing false in him' (7:18). Some thought that Jesus was mad—a demon had possessed him (7:20)—and in reply Jesus referred to a previous discussion about the sabbath (as in 5:1–18).

The thrust of the controversy of course was about the true identity of Jesus. The tension developed as armed police came to arrest him. Misunderstandings and arguments persisted but Jesus was beyond their reach. His death will not come at this whim of the authorities because—here it is again—his 'hour' had not yet come (7:30). Then, on the last great day of the festival, Jesus was revealed as the source of the living water of the Spirit (7:37–38) and the light of the world (8:12). This did not end disputes and questions, but at the end of Chapter 8 Jesus was unharmed by threats of stoning and was able to hide himself and walk safely out of the temple.

So much Christology is contained in these two chapters, 7 and 8. We cannot fail to see that Jesus' words and actions—so full of conflict and requiring much courage from Jesus—invite hearers to make a choice. If they believe in him they will find authentic freedom: 'the truth shall make you free' (8:31–38). True disciples will be free with God, who knows and loves them.

The twists and turns of this controversy may confuse us but the message is clear. Jesus unsettles all worldly relationships, such as in his own family, and questions long-held theological certainties, such as those that the 'Jews' held about Moses and the law. He comes from 'above' whereas they are 'from below'. The crowd, the authorities (such as the Pharisees and chief priests), and Jesus are in conflict. Only Nicodemus, a Pharisee himself, is able to break their fierce determination to take Jesus and destroy him without any trial (7:50–52).

What may we learn from all this conflict, misunderstanding and confrontation? It has been summarised as this: 'God presented in the Gospel means an agonising exposure of human evasiveness in all its forms'.[13] Every possible strategy was employed to divert Jesus from his mission. His brothers evidently wanted him to continue to perform miraculous 'signs' so that they could bask in reflected glory. Others wanted to see Jesus simply as 'a good man' (7:12), 'a performer of signs' (7:31), the 'prophet' or even the Messiah (7:40–41), but he certainly was a compelling speaker (7:46).

There were others who dismissed him as a deceiver (7:12), an ignoramus (7:15), a pretentious proselytiser (7:35), unaccredited (8:13) and of dubious origins (7:41; 8:19), as suicidal (8:22), a Samaritan (8:48), as one possessed (7:20, 8:48), a deluded visionary (8:57), as deserving both arrest (7:30, 32, 43, 45) and the penalty for blasphemy (8:59).[14]

The coming of Jesus to the world created and still provokes a variety of responses. His coming changed the world that had been. If what Jesus claimed is true then it is a profound challenge to every person and their understanding of their identity and purpose in the world. Do we believe that the Father is revealed by Jesus and that this challenges us as to how we should live?

There remains the challenge to every reader of John: can we see ourselves among the range of responses to Jesus? We can also become as indifferent or resistant to the gift of eternal life as those who confronted the human Jesus. Do we really believe? Have we been open to the transforming love of God in Jesus? Are we then able to follow him to our destiny as children of God?

BEING IN THE FAMILY OF JESUS

As we think about the brothers and sisters of Jesus we may find special comfort and challenge in what Jesus said when he was told that his family wanted to draw him away from his mission. He pointed to his disciples and said: 'Here are my mother and my brothers! Whoever does the will of my father in heaven is my brother and sister and mother' (Matthew 12:49–50). Believers are all in the family!

To be born again is to be born into this special family. Despite all the tensions and distractions that can sometimes happen in church life, there is this supreme privilege of family, of belonging. In the early church they greeted each other as 'sister' or 'brother' and whilst this has sometimes become a rather sentimental and hackneyed greeting, the reality of belonging to what the apostle called 'the household of God' (Ephesians 2:19) remains a source of unfailing support and identity.

Questions for discussion

1. Study the references to the family of Jesus as given in this chapter. What are your main impressions, and are there ways in which these can help us in our family relations? Why do you think there is really so little information about the earthly family of Jesus in the gospels?

2. Discuss the ways in which your family and circle of friends have helped or hindered your witness. How should we react to family members who are not Christians and who may ridicule our faith?

3. Can you reconcile what Jesus told his brothers and his later action in actually going to Jerusalem? What might we learn from this?

4. What do you understand by the statement of Jesus that this was not his *kairos* moment? Can you think of any personal or family circumstances that might be described as having been such a *kairos* moment for you?

5. Note the various ways in which hearers responded to Jesus in these two chapters (7 and 8). Can you identify any modern parallels to these responses? How should we react to any of these?

6. In what sense may we understand ourselves as being in the family of God through our faith in Jesus? Can you share times when that sense of belonging has been helpful and important for you?

7. Discuss the ways in which the temptations of Jesus in the wilderness are also found in this story. What does this suggest about the life of Jesus?

1. A key character in Dan Brown's blockbuster novel *The Da Vinci Code* is revealed to be descended from Jesus: see the novels listed at https://en.wikipedia.org/w/index php brothers of Jesus, accessed 2 October 2016.
2. BF Westcott, *The Gospel According to St John* (London: John Murray, 1919), p. 115.
3. As cited by L Morris, *The Gospel According to John* (Grand Rapids: Eerdmans, 1977), p. 394.
4. A Plummer, as cited by Morris, *John*, p. 394.
5. L Newbigin, *The Light Has Come* (Grand Rapids: Eerdmans, 1982), p. 93.
6. FB Craddock, *John* (Atlanta; John Knox Press, 1982), p. 58.
7. Calvin, as cited by FD Bruner, *The Gospel of John. A Commentary* (Grand Rapids: Eerdmans, 2012), p. 468.
8. Morris, *John*, pp. 396–97.
9. For Dorothy see JR Beck, *Dorothy Carey. The Tragic and Untold Story of Mrs William Carey* (Grand Rapids: Baker, 1992).
10. CS Keener, *The Gospel of John: A Commentary* (2 vols; Grand Rapids: Baker, 2003), vol 1, p. 710.
11. Westcott, *The Gospel According to St John*, p. 115.
12. R Brown, *The Gospel According to John* (3 vols; New York: Doubleday, 1966), vol 1, p. 308.
13. AJ Kelly and FJ Moloney, *Experiencing God in the Gospel of John* (New York: Paulist Press, 2003), p. 199.
14. See Kelly and Moloney, *Experiencing God*, pp. 199–200.

'The Light of the World', William Holman Hunt, 1851–1853

CHAPTER SEVEN

KNOWING WHO I AM: JESUS AND 'THE JEWS'
(JOHN 8:12–59)

This long chapter raises a painful and difficult issue, what James Dunn has called 'the embarrassment of history'[1]—the problem of 'anti-Judaism' in John. A crucial verse is 8:44 where Jesus called the Jews 'children of the devil'. Martin Luther, whom we revere as the bold and courageous reformer, later in life engaged in vulgar and vigorous polemics against the Jews, aided by this verse and the cry of the Jews in Matthew 27:25: 'His blood be on us and on our children!'

What can we make of these 'texts of terror'[2] that have been employed in the appalling anti-Semitism that has marked much of the church's history, especially during the Middle Ages when Jews were persecuted as 'Christ-killers'? German Nazis also used this verse to justify their virulent anti-Semitism, which led to the appalling horrors of the Holocaust.

In order to grapple with these complex issues, we need first to look closely at this chapter as a whole. The crucial verse of 8:44 should not be taken out of context and read in an ethnic way. The thought seems to skip and jump about and is not easy to summarise, although the question of origins is significant—Jesus is 'from above' but the Jews are 'from below' (8:23)—and their father is the devil. Here is the crux of the controversy.

JESUS AS THE LIGHT OF THE WORLD ENGAGES WITH REPRESENTATIVES OF DARKNESS

READ 8:12–20

It seems that Jesus was still at the festival and on this occasion was speaking in the 'treasury of the temple' (8:20), which was that section of the temple precinct into which people came to cast their offerings into the trumpet-shaped collection boxes that were placed there. As this was a public place it was possible for Jesus to teach there. It was also dangerous, in that the temple police were nearby; but as John stresses—in his familiar way—they ignored Jesus 'because his hour had not yet come' (8:20).

The central question was posed by his hearers: 'Who are you anyway?' (8:25). To raise this fundamental issue, John traces a tense conversation that begins with the startling and comprehensive claim by Jesus: 'I am the light of the world'.

Light is if course one of the dominant themes in John, often linked with life, as here (see 1:4–5). That is what this great controversy is really about: the struggle between light and darkness, between life and death. Light is the means to see other realities, but light is known only by itself. This 'I am' claim by Jesus asserts both exclusivity—that Jesus is *the* light—and inclusivity in its scope of being *for the world*. This remarkable claim by Jesus has brought purpose and direction to countless believers: 'in him was the light of all people' (1:4). At the same time, this chapter reveals a dark and menacing reality: the world cannot see the light that is shining before it.

The response of the Pharisees was not to focus on the actual claim but to raise a legal point about the credibility of any claim that is not supported by more than one witness. Jesus insisted that he was able to validate his claims because of his origins and identity (8:14), whilst his hearers were able to judge solely by human standards. Jesus also claimed that he and the Father who sent him are one, and so there is a sense in which he has two witnesses. As so often in John, Jesus' cryptic answer was misunderstood and applied on a human level. 'Where is your father?' they demanded. To which Jesus simply offered another puzzling and doubtless infuriating response: 'If you really knew me you would also know the father' (8:19).

READ 8:21–30

Again, Jesus' words were misunderstood. He told them that he was going away and they would not be able to follow him. Readers of the gospel will know that Jesus later said much the same thing to his disciples in the upper room (13:33) but here the Jews not unreasonably think that Jesus implied that he was about to leave them by suicide; that certainly would be a place where they would not be able to go (8:22). Jesus elaborates that they are from below, from this world, and that they will die for their sin. This word is singular in 8:21—it is not particular sins that they might commit but sin in the sense that they do not believe in him (8:24).

This provokes the puzzled and vital question: 'Then, who on earth are you?' But of course the claim of Jesus was that he was not simply 'on earth' in terms of origins and identity. The refrain is repeated: 'They did not understand' (8:27). That Jesus was uniquely and definitively the one sent from the Father is again asserted.

READ: 8:31–38

What is important to notice is that this conversation led some of his hearers to believe in him (8:30). So, in all that follows, Jesus spoke to 'the Jews who had believed in him' (8:31). This raises some problems for readers because it is these

Jewish 'believers' who are later criticised and condemned in the ensuing passage. How did these Jewish 'believers' turn out to be so hostile to Jesus?

Jesus gave a fundamental principle for all believers: they will truly be his disciples if they 'continue in' or 'abide' or 'make a home' in his word (8:31). Continuing in the faith is crucial. It is not enough simply to express some interest and a kind of intellectual assent to what Jesus said. The challenge is to live in the word of Christ, and this entails a perpetual listening and obedience to what one hears. As William Temple wrote: 'To go so far and then stop is a sign of very grave spiritual trouble'.[3] For John this is a spiritual failure, and leads to a hardening and a bitter rejection of who Jesus really is.

Only the word of Jesus is truth and only this truth brings spiritual freedom. The Zealots of Jesus' day thought that they could bring political freedom from Rome by their violence and guerrilla tactics. But Jesus taught that nothing else can bring absolute freedom but the gospel, which offers freedom from our greatest bondage, that of sin (8:34–36).

READ 8:39–47

This is the longest and hardest section in these chapters, and includes one of the most unpleasant exchanges in John, including the accusation that the Jews are children of the devil. The real theme is Abraham. The biblical Abraham was a pilgrim of faith, but these Jews have made him a kind of identity badge to be flashed at anyone who disturbed their theological dogmas.

Jesus seems to taunt his hearers by observing that they are descendants of Abraham yet are looking to kill him. Jesus does not deny their physical descent from Abraham but condemns their conduct—especially their determination to reject the one who has brought the truth—and reveals that they have another paternity that shapes their rejection of Jesus and his word. To their indignant retort that as children of Abraham they have never been slaves to anyone, Jesus shows that they are indeed slaves of sin, recalling the language of Paul in Romans 6.

The Jews insist that they are true children of Abraham and seem to repeat a common slur against Jesus that he was born out of wedlock—was an illegitimate child. Unlike Jesus, they argue, we are legitimate children of father Abraham, and, moreover, children of the one true God (8:41). Jesus' reply is amazing: 'I am here. I have come from God who sent me!' (8:42).

But Jesus now attacks them in a sharp way. The devil deals in lies and death, and by not believing the truth when it is right in front of them—in Jesus—these Jews show that this is the awful family to whom they belong. The words of Jesus in 8:44 come in one of the longest verses in the whole gospel and also the harshest. For the first time in John, Jesus asserts that the real opposition against him comes from the devil and those who belong to him. This is repeated again and again (see 12:31; 14:30; 16:11, 17:15). Only those who are from God hear the words of God (8:47).

READ 8:48–59

The retorts and insults continued. The Jews charged Jesus with being a Samaritan and having a demon. Jesus did not linger to comment on the absurd charge that he was a Samaritan, and then simply refuted the accusation that he was possessed by a demon. Jesus proceeded to show that in all that he said and did he honoured his Father.

Again, a word of Jesus provoked his hearers. He claimed that all who kept his word would never 'see death' (8:51). The retort was immediate: you must be mad, since Abraham and all the prophets died! Are you saying you are greater than all of these whom we honour in our faith? Temple suggests that Jesus' words should be translated: 'will not notice death'. He was not declaring that his followers would not die but that it would be a kind of 'physical incident', that it would be irrelevant to their faith and identity. 'Though it will happen to him, it will matter to him no more than the fall of a leaf from a tree under which he might be reading a book. It happens to him, but he does not in any full sense see or notice it'.[4]

But there was more to come from Jesus. He told his astonished hearers that Abraham rejoiced that he had been able to see the day of Jesus (8:56). This once again was misunderstood in a crude literalistic way: 'You are not yet fifty years old! But Abraham lived hundreds of years ago!' Jesus was not wishing to engage with them in any sort of absurd discussions about time travel, and recognised that they were in what has been termed 'their frozen pattern of incomprehension'.[5]

What was Jesus saying? Simply, that Abraham understood that he was not the fulfilment of the promises of God but looked forward in faith to the day of the Messiah. So Jesus was claiming to be that promised figure.

So the cacophony of conflict and contention continued. Then came the ultimate claim of Jesus: 'Before Abraham was, I am' (8:58). This so offended his hearers that they picked up stones and tried to kill him as the appropriate punishment for blasphemy. Certainly this was an extraordinary claim made by Jesus. Notice that Jesus did not say, 'Before Abraham was, I was'. 'I am' was of course the sacred name of God in the Old Testament (YHWH) and one that John shows Jesus using on several occasions (see 13:19). It was a claim to divinity, although it is made by 'allusion and implication'.[6]

Once again we too cannot avoid the question: Was Jesus mad? Was he a deluded blasphemer? Or was he, in very truth, God 'made flesh' in our midst? As Stauffer well says of Jesus' meaning: 'Where I am, there is God, there God lives, speaks, calls, asks, acts, decides, loves, chooses, forgives, rejects, hardens, suffers, dies'.[7]

WHO ARE 'THE JEWS' IN JOHN'S GOSPEL?

We need to return to the problem which we identified at the beginning of this chapter and the way in which these verses (especially 8:44) have been used to justify racism and anti-Semitic violence. As Pope John Paul II declared in 1998: 'In the Christian world—I do not say on the part of the Church as such—erroneous and unjust interpretations of the New Testament regarding the Jewish people and their alleged culpability have circulated for too long, engendering feelings of hostility towards this people'.[8]

The word 'Jews' is regularly used in John, and about half of the seventy uses are hostile or critical. Not all are negative, notably in the chapter about Jesus and the Samaritan woman in which Jesus declares that 'salvation is from the Jews' (4:22).

James Dunn has emphasised that first century Judaism was a factionalised group. Some were extremely critical towards other groups and 'Judaism' was often severely divided. For example, the Qumran community was highly critical of the priests in Jerusalem. This means that when we ask, 'Was John anti-Judaism?' we are obliged to ask, 'Which Judaism?' It was more like something of an intense family row. Dunn adds that it is important initially to hear these words with first century ears and 'not with twentieth century sensitivities'.[9]

This kind of extreme language between adherents of the same religion is not simply an ancient reality. The way in which, for example, certain 'liberals' and 'fundamentalists' within Christendom sometimes speak of each other is scarcely less edifying.

Indeed, it is also important to understand how difficult it was for Jews to convert to Christianity by the time that John was written:

> Modern scholars sometimes leave the impression that a Jewish believer in Jesus could leave Judaism as easily as a person can today leave, let us say, the Methodist Church for the Episcopalian … But … to leave Judaism meant to move from one society to another; it involved the painful severing not only of family and cultic ties but being cut off from the whole life of a community upon which one was socially and economically dependent.[10]

This understanding has guided contemporary mission activity among, for example, Muslim communities.

The destruction of Jerusalem in 70 CE was a major turning point in the history of the Jewish people and certainly in Jewish–Christian relations. Yet even as early as, say, Acts and Galatians, we can discern the impact of 'Judaisers' on the early Christian communities. Dunn's view is that John reflects an inner-Jewish—thus not anti-Jewish—conflict. We should not, then, imagine two monoliths—Judaism and Christianity—denouncing one another.

This does not solve our problem. As DJ Harrington observes:

> The basic problem … is that John's gospel says nasty things about a group that it calls 'the Jews'. When twentieth century people hear such negative talk about 'the Jews', they may assume a direct relation between 'the Jews' of the Fourth Gospel and their Jewish neighbours who attend the local synagogue. Thus the Fourth Gospel can become a vehicle for increasing anti-Semitism.[11]

R E Brown has rightly observed that even if a modern day Christian would never use the phrase that the Jews are 'children of the devil' it does not help contemporary Jewish–Christian relationships to disguise the fact that such an attitude once existed.[12]

Many scholars regard 'the Jews' in John as referring simply to Judean Jewish leaders and certainly not all Jewish believers. Jesus and his disciples were all Jewish. We noted in the previous chapter how John referred to Jewish people at a Jewish festival who dared not speak about Jesus because of 'fear of the Jews' (7:13)!

This also raises questions about interpretation and the translation of the Bible. Earlier generations used Scripture to justify slavery and racism. We need to be open to new insights and understandings of Scripture. The concept of 'dynamic equivalence' has helped many Bible translators in conveying the Bible's message to people who have no vocabulary to translate a biblical concept. Some have suggested, therefore, that 'the Jews' should be translated by such terms as 'the Jewish authorities'; this was the approach of the American Bible Society in its *Contemporary English Version* (1995). This does help us understand the way in which John refers to Jesus' opponents.

CONCLUSION

This passage invites careful thought about how we should engage with Jewish people today. Some Christian organisations have an aggressive approach to seeking the conversion of Jews whilst others engage in a more thoughtful dialogue which respects traditional Jewish beliefs.[13] In some ways the existence of Israel as a political state complicates dialogue between Christians and Jews today since any criticism of the Israeli nation can be so twisted as to be thought of as anti-Semitic.

We should be careful not to let our justifiable questions of interpretation about 'the Jews' distract us from the personal challenges of this chapter. We must in a sense forget about who the Jews were and ask ourselves whether we really are true believers. Recall that these opponents were all students of their Bible and devoted to their theological traditions. With our own precise beliefs and loved practices, we can also slip into deserving these awesome rebukes of Jesus. Not only any modern Jews who may read this, but we ourselves, are pierced by the startling words of Jesus. Do we believe that Jesus is indeed 'the light of the world', that he is the Son of God come in human flesh? What difference would it make to our living if we truly believed all this about Jesus? Have we become opponents of what Jesus is doing in our world?

The following challenge captures this question and each of us must offer a personal response:

> Whether we be Christians or Jews, priests, theologians, laity, or church authorities, or anyone else in the great drama of human history, a hermeneutic of humility is in order. It is possible for all of us, or any of us at different times, to be contributing to the culture of Antichrist, as it infects our history and relationships with one another with a murderous lie, to cause the self-centredness that makes us either indifferent or resistant to the gift of the life-transforming revelation of God in Christ.[14]

Questions for discussion

1. What exactly does it mean to you to affirm that Jesus is the 'Light of the World'?

2. Review the conflict as recorded in John 8. What are your main impressions? What do these verses reveal about the claims of Jesus and the rejection of these by his hearers? Can you identify any modern parallels?

3. Explore the comments about believers who do not continue in the faith (8:31–32). Is this a modern problem, and, if so, how would you apply the words of Jesus to this situation?

4. Precisely what is meant by Jesus accusing the Jews who rejected him as 'children of the devil'? Is this type of criticism ever relevant today?

5. What do you understand by the words of Jesus in 8:51, that those who keep his word 'will never taste death'?

6. Discuss the different understandings about the role of Abraham in this exchange. Can you identify any other New Testament passages where Abraham is a central figure in the discussion?

7. How helpful or justifiable is it to translate 'the Jews' as 'Jewish authorities'?

8. How would you respond to a Jewish friend who claimed that the teachings of Jesus led to the anti-Semitism that has been such a sad feature of Jewish history? (Share any personal experiences you may have had on this issue.)

9. List the spiritual insights and challenges that you find in this chapter. In particular, how do you respond to the quotation with which this study concludes?

Knowing who I am: Jesus and 'the Jews'

1. JDG Dunn, 'The Embarrassment of History: Reflections on the Problem of "Anti-Judaism" in the Fourth Gospel', in R Beiringer, D Pollefeyt and F Vandecasteele-Vanneuville (eds), *Anti-Judaism and the Fourth Gospel* (Assen: Royal van Gorcum, 2001), pp. 47–67.
2. Phyllis Trible, as cited by the editors in *Anti-Judaism and the Fourth Gospel,* p. 43.
3. W Temple, *Readings in St John's Gospel* (London; Macmillan, 1961), p. 136.
4. Temple, *Readings in St John's Gospel,* p. 142.
5. AJ Kelly and FJ Moloney, *Experiencing God in the Gospel of John* (New York: Paulist Press, 2003), p. 198.
6. Temple, *Readings in St John's Gospel,* pp. 149–50.
7. E Stauffer as cited by L Morris, *The Gospel According to John* (Grand Rapids: Eerdmans, 1973), p. 474.
8. Pope John Paul II as cited by editors in *Anti-Judaism and the Fourth Gospel,* p. 5.
9. Dunn, 'The Embarrassment of History', p. 58.
10. Davies and Allison as cited by CS Keener, *The Gospel of John: A Commentary* (Grand Rapids: Baker, 2003), vol 1, p. 215.
11. DJ Harrington as cited by JH Charlesworth, 'The Gospel of John: Exclusivism caused by a social setting different from that of Jesus (John 11:54 and 14:6)', in *Anti-Judaism and the Fourth Gospel,* p. 480.
12. R E Brown, as cited by editors in *Anti-Judaism and the Fourth Gospel,* p. 37.
13. For example, the Council of Christians and Jews in Victoria includes in its aims: 'to educate Christians and Jews to appreciate each other's distinctive beliefs, practices and commonalities'.
14. Kelly and Moloney, *Experiencing God in the Gospel of John,* p. 203.

'Last Supper', Wissington Suffolk, 13th century

CHAPTER EIGHT

THE CROOKED TREASURER: JESUS AND JUDAS
(JOHN 13:21-30)

Many people met Jesus. A select few were included in his inner circle, the twelve disciples. Surely these were the most privileged: to be with him day and night, to see how he changed peoples' lives, to hear his matchless and inspiring teaching. These intimate experiences surely must have shaped their thinking and living. Yes, at times it was difficult—they became tired and disillusioned, they often misunderstood what Jesus was saying and doing—but what a special and unique privilege! Later generations envy all those selected to be in that inner circle with Jesus.

But then we think about Judas! He was one of that chosen twelve and shared in all the excitement of those early days with Jesus. How then did Judas become the one who handed Jesus over to those who killed him? His name has become a symbol of heinous betrayal, so that, as George Buttrick once observed, 'We would not name a child, or even a dog "Judas"'.[1]

We cannot avoid the challenge of this encounter between Jesus and Judas, even if the story bristles with difficulties and ambiguities. Every encounter with Jesus, even this ultimately tragic one, invites us to reflect on our own relationship with him.

Judas has become a major problem of history and theology, one that has intrigued and divided preachers and scholars across the ages. Interest has increased in recent years with the publication of the *Gospel of Judas*, a Gnostic text which has provoked some bizarre reinterpretations of his place in Christian history. Was he alone entrusted with a secret and true understanding of Jesus? Church leaders were obliged to reject these claims, as Archbishop Rowan Williams did in his 2006 Easter address: 'This is a demonstrably late text which simply parallels a large number of quite well-known works from the more eccentric fringes of the early Church'.[2]

Popular fiction, dramatic plays, and the popular musical *Jesus Christ Superstar* have all featured Judas prominently. The fascination is seemingly endless. Bernard Dieckmann has summarised the reason for this phenomenon: 'Judas has not been a marginal figure in Christendom. He presents us with a central human and Christian problem: how to deal with the enemy, the foreigner, and our understanding of evil'.[3]

Certainly Judas is a central figure in the gospels. Of the twelve, only Peter is mentioned more often than Judas. Many questions persist. How could Judas do what he did? Even more problematically, what exactly did Judas do and what were his motives? Was he so controlled by evil (Satan) that he did not know what he was doing? Was his role foretold in scripture so that his act was predetermined? How can we reconcile seemingly conflicting accounts of his death?

John features Judas at five places in his gospel and an examination of these will lead us to central questions of interpretation about him.

JOHN 6:64–71

This incident came after the miraculous feeding of the crowd and reports how, in response to some of Jesus' teaching, many began to 'turn back'. Jesus asked if the twelve would also leave. Simon Peter's reply was to confess that they could not go anywhere else as they had found in Jesus 'the words of eternal life', and that they believed that he was 'the holy one of God'. Jesus then replied that he had indeed chosen these disciples but then added the solemn note: 'Yet one of you is a devil' (6:70).

This is the first mention of the betrayal by John, and so he added a note: 'He was speaking of Judas son of Simon Iscariot for he, though one of the twelve, was going to betray him' (6:71).

Several points are made. First, Jesus chose Judas—he was one of the twelve. Did Jesus know about the true character of his disciple? Dorothy Sayers rightly reminds us: 'One thing is certain: he cannot have been the creeping, crawling, patently worthless villain that some simple-minded people would like to make out; that would be to cast too grave a slur upon the brains and character of Jesus'.[4]

He is here described as Judas, the son of Simon Iscariot. Judas was a very common name among Jewish families. Iscariot is most commonly thought to refer to his town of origin—Kerioth in Judea—although the exact location is disputed. He was thus the only disciple not from Galilee. Some suggest that the name could be linked with the 'Sicarii' (dagger-men), a term used by Josephus to disparage those assassins associated with the Zealots who sought deliverance by force. Of course another of the disciples was Simon the Zealot. We simply cannot be sure what the description of Judas means.

This reference to the unbelief of Judas so early in the ministry of Jesus is unique and reflects the emphasis in this gospel that Jesus was not taken by surprise: 'He knew from the start those who would not believe and would hand him over' (6:64). The fragility of human response to Jesus has always been present. In Matthew and Mark, when Peter tried to dissuade Jesus from the path of suffering, he was rebuked: 'Get behind me Satan' (Matthew 16:13 // Mark 8:33). John does not record this exchange but rather directs attention to the one who is 'a devil'. Jesus does not name Judas, but John does. Unbelief cannot remain permanently hidden and these stories show how close Peter and Judas really were: 'How near the saint is to the sinner', observed William Temple.[5]

JOHN 12:1–8

This beautiful story of devotion towards Jesus is marred by the shrill complaint of Judas about the waste of the expensive ointment so lovingly lavished on Jesus. The fragrance filled the whole house but only Judas criticises 'the waste'. Judas is simply designated as 'the one who was about to betray him'. John informs the reader that Judas was a hypocrite when he claimed that the money could have been given to the poor—Judas was treasurer for the disciples—since he actually wanted the money for himself. John unambiguously declares that Judas was a thief. Greed has overtaken him even as the aroma of a selfless sacrifice filled his senses. What self-justification even the basest of thieves can make in their own defence!

Judas' claim for what we might now call 'social justice'—his hypocritical concern for the poor—is a pitiful deceit. He represents those whom Jesus had earlier described as 'hired hands' who do not care for the sheep but only for the dishonest gains they can make (John 10:12–13). Presumably he had hoped to benefit from the gifts that well-intentioned supporters gave to Jesus and his men. As Westcott noticed, temptation commonly comes through that for which we are naturally fitted.[6] Judas was good with accounting and money and this was where he failed. Sadly, he was not the last to fail in this precise way within church communities.

The reply of Jesus that we would always have the poor with us cannot be employed to suggest that Christians do not, therefore, have to serve the needy. Simply to recall the story about the Good Samaritan is to give a lie to any self-seeking excuse for our failures to serve the needy with compassion and sacrifice.

JOHN 13:1–30

This matchless scene is etched into the hearts of all believers. Jesus knew that at last his hour had come, the hour of his departure, the hour of his betrayal and death. With deep emotion John insists that Jesus had loved his own who were in the world, indeed 'loved them to the end' (13:1). Immediately follows the sad observation that, notwithstanding this enduring love of Jesus, there was a dark force in that upper room: 'The devil had already put it into the heart of Judas … to betray him' (13:2). The word 'betray' literally means 'to hand over'. The ultimate force at work is clearly the devil or Satan (13:27). The disciples would be indwelt by the Father and Jesus (14:20, 23) but Judas welcomed another, evil, force into his life. Judas was not exonerated from the act he undertook. Here we find a blend of personal human responsibility—Judas permitting and welcoming this evil power—and the ultimate Evil One who is determined to overthrow what God is doing in the world. Still, there should be no doubt that the ultimate responsibility for the cosmic significance of these events lay with Satan.

The washing of the disciples' feet is a moving moment of humility by Jesus when his service for all humankind is depicted. Judas seems to have been the special object of a last loving appeal from Jesus. The betrayal comes in the context of an intimate scene. Jesus loved each one of them to the end, and the foot-washing had occurred with John stressing the full knowledge of Jesus that the Father had given all things to him and that he had come from God and now was going to God. With that priceless sense of unique identity, what did Jesus do? He wrapped a towel around him, knelt before each man and washed his smelly feet. Peter queried whether Jesus should wash his feet but no such murmur came from Judas. Jesus, however, told Peter that not all of them were clean, 'for he knew who was to betray him'.

What was Judas thinking as Jesus carefully washed each dirty foot? No one can really know. Many are convinced that Judas had already resolved to betray Jesus because he had come to believe that Jesus was taking the wrong path; if only he could arrange for Jesus to meet with the chief priests he could then persuade them somehow to give up trying to kill him. They would be forced to listen to him firsthand. That would make the difference. Perhaps Jesus could even persuade them to stand up against the Romans?

Who knows what Judas thought? Pearce Carey imagined the mind of Judas: 'He craved a Soldier, not a Servant; a Christ of masterhood, not meekness; of sceptre and crown, not of basin and towel'.[7] Did Jesus still see all the gifts and promise that Judas had shown when first he asked him to follow him?

We can be even more certain of how much Jesus still loved Judas by the tender scene when they were reclining at the last supper. There were hints, if only Judas could detect them. Jesus spoke openly. There is one who has shared bread with me and yet has 'lifted up his heel against me' (13:18), a practice still of a highly offensive nature in Eastern custom. Jesus was terribly distressed as the awful moment of betrayal came closer (13:21). Could he not bring Judas back to him? The other gospels portray all the disciples asking, 'Is it I?' In John, Jesus whispered to one of the disciples that the betrayer was 'the one to whom I give this piece of bread', the tasty morsel, a special gift offered to a special friend. A last look and Jesus, seeing the blank look and averted eyes of Judas, gave the urgent command, 'Go and do it quickly!' (If only Judas had obeyed other commands of Jesus!) This cryptic order protected Judas from the inevitable hostility of the others: Judas evidently was often asked to undertake practical tasks for the group.

John simply remembers: 'It was night'. This was 'the night on which he was betrayed' (1 Cor. 11:23). Judas went out from the intimacy and conviviality of that room and that presence. The Light still shone in that upper room. Outside, it was black and nothing more of Judas could be seen at that point.

JOHN 17:12

Even in the special priestly prayer of Jesus (to be discussed in the next chapter) there is one reference to Judas. Jesus rejoices with the Father that not one of his chosen ones is lost, 'except the one destined to be lost', which could be translated as 'the son of destruction'. This exact phrase is used in an apocalyptic sense in 2

Thessalonians 2:3. This element of predestination provokes the question: Was Judas free to take any other course? If his act and its consequence were foretold, was Judas some kind of automaton and not a free and willing person? Which particular Old Testament text might have been in mind is not certain, possibly Psalm 41:9: 'Even my bosom friend in whom I trusted, who ate my bread, has lifted the heel against me'.

Calvin wisely commented: 'It would be wrong for anyone to infer … that Judas' fall should be imputed to God rather than to himself, in that necessity was laid on him by prophecy'.[8]

JOHN 18:1–11

Judas' role in the actual betrayal is not as detailed in John. There is no mention of the agony in the garden, no thirty pieces of silver, no identifying kiss, no subsequent remorse leading to the death of Judas. He was clearly named as the one who handed Jesus over (18:5) to the Jewish authorities and the Romans who came with them. Indeed, in the Greek the verb is in the present tense, suggesting that Judas at that exact moment was betraying Jesus. He had taken sides and there was no turning back: he was 'standing with them'.

With dramatic irony John depicts Judas, the soldiers and officials coming out of the dark night with their lanterns and torches and weapons to confront the Light of the World. Jesus replied to the query about his identity—'I am he'—and readers of the gospel will know that this phrase clearly placed him on the holy ground of divine revelation (Exodus 3:5).

Judas is not mentioned again in John's gospel. Matthew tells us about the remorse of Judas and how he brought back the thirty pieces of silver, and after the officials refused to take his money he threw the coins at them, went out and hanged himself. The authorities used his money to buy a potter's field for use as a cemetery in which to bury foreigners (Matthew 27:3–10). Acts claims that the money was used by Judas to buy the field but there he fell headlong, 'burst open in the middle and all his bowels gushed out' (Acts 1:15–20). These two accounts seem to conflict, although many attempts have been made to reconcile them.

John does not pursue these tragic events but is nonetheless realistic about the horror of what Judas did. Judas remains a figure of fascination and various interpretations. Dante, 'judging sins by their temperature and reckoning cold-blooded treachery worse than sins of passion', set Judas not in hell's central fire, but in its lowest pool of eternal ice.[9]

The modern believer who wishes to remain true to how Scripture portrays Judas will notice how Jesus tried to love Judas into returning to being a faithful disciple. Perhaps his dramatic end, as Matthew and Luke record his fate, is a sign of a deep repentance. Origen thought that Judas rushed into the world of the dead to meet Christ there and to entreat his forgiveness. Who can say?

William Klassen concludes his comprehensive discussion of whether Judas was the betrayer or a friend of Jesus with an imaginative 'suicide note' from Judas. 'Judas' writes as he realises that Jesus has been handed over to the Romans:

> I am at my wits end and I do not know which way to turn. My heart has turned to water. What made our high priest turn our Lord over to the Romans? … What is left for me to do? …
>
> I have agonized over whether I should die with him. He often said the disciple is not above his master and that we must suffer with him. If our Lord dies, there is no honour greater than to die with him.
>
> I am terribly frightened, sad and troubled. I never had all this in mind. Who would ever have thought that the kingdom of God could end this way. If Jesus dies on the cross, surely he cannot be the Messiah …
>
> Now I will die with him. For the sake of my wife and children, let this act of taking my own life also be seen in the light of my love for my master. If he dies, I want to die with him.[10]

FB Craddock also offers a sober and thoughtful challenge to all modern interpreters of Judas:

> Rather than speculating on the reasons for his act (love of money, political disappointment, attempting to provoke Jesus into a move against the establishment, schizophrenia, demon possession, etc) the church would better spend its time responding as Mark says the twelve did: 'They began to be sorrowful, and to say to him one after another, "Is it I?" (Mark: 14:19)[11]

Still today we need to ask the same question and reaffirm our unending love for the one who died for us.

Questions for discussion

1. Why do you think Judas has remained such an intriguing figure, and the focus of so many different interpretations?

2. Do you find it helpful to think of Judas as 'handing over' Jesus to the authorities rather than betraying him? What do you think is the difference?

3. Discuss how we can understand Judas being 'a devil' and yet having human responsibilities. In what sense can we speak of someone or some movement being 'Satanic'? What are the advantages or dangers in using language like this?

4. Discuss the observation of Westcott that our failures are often linked with our special giftedness.

5. What exactly do you think Jesus meant by saying that we will always have the poor with us?

6. Imagine being at the last supper and seeing Jesus wash the feet of the disciples. What do you think Jesus meant by doing this? What could it have meant to Judas?

7. Read the extracts from the imaginary suicide note of Judas and discuss the ideas presented there.

8. Discuss the quotation from Craddock with which the chapter is concluded.

9. What is your considered conclusion about the character and fate of Judas?

The crooked treasurer: Jesus and Judas

1. G Buttrick, as cited by W Klassen, *Judas Betrayer or Friend of Jesus?* (London: SCM Press, 1996), p. 29.
2. See E Pagels, *Reading Judas: The Gospel of Judas and the Shaping of Christianity* (New York: Viking, 2007); MW Meyer, *Judas: The Definitive Collection of Gospels and Legends About the Infamous Apostle of Jesus* (New York: Harper, 2007); NT Wright, *Judas and the Gospel of Jesus: Have We Missed the Truth About Christianity?* (London: SPCK, 2006).
3. B Dieckmann, as cited by Klassen, *Judas Betrayer or Friend of Jesus?*, p. 1.
4. D Sayers, *The Man Born to be King* (London: Victor Gollancz, 1942), p. 30.
5. W Temple, *Readings in St John's Gospel* (London: Macmillan, 1961), p. 99.
6. BF Westcott, *The Gospel According to St John* (London: John Murray, 1919), p. 177.
7. SP Carey, *Jesus and Judas* (New York: Richard Smith, 1931), p. 122.
8. J Calvin, as cited by L Morris, *The Gospel According to John* (Grand Rapids: Eerdmans, 1971), p. 728.
9. Carey, *Jesus and Judas*, p. 233.
10. Klassen *Judas Betrayer or Friend of Jesus?*, pp. 205–207.
11. FB Craddock, *John* (Atlanta: John Knox Press, 1982), p. 102.

'Agony in the Garden', Giovanni Bellini, c. 1459

CHAPTER NINE

THOSE WHO WILL BELIEVE IN ME: JESUS AND THE BELIEVERS OF ALL AGES
(JOHN 17:1–26)

This chapter moves us into a new kind of encounter with Jesus, one that in the most direct and intimate way concerns believers of all time. Jesus here prays quite specifically for all those who, like us today, have become believers because of the witness of the apostles and countless millions across the ages (17:20). Yes, the incredible affirmation is that Jesus prayed and still prays for us!

To know that someone else is praying for you is an incredible encouragement. One of my most embarrassing and humbling encounters took place some years ago when I was visiting a sick friend in our local hospital. To my surprise this friend said discreetly: 'Do you know the lady over in that bed?' I glanced across and whispered: 'I don't think so'. The reply came: 'She says that she knows you'. Naturally I went to speak with this patient and to my surprise was greeted with the astonishing affirmation: 'I know you don't remember me, but when you were a student you preached at our little church. And I was moved by what you said and I told you then that I would pray for you every day that God would bless your ministry'. She added quietly: 'And I have done so. Every day. It is so good to see you again and to hear about your work'. You can imagine how I felt. It must have been something like twenty-five years! I still marvel at this extraordinary gift of an otherwise unknown friend.

Yet, how much more to know that Jesus prays for us!

JESUS 'ON THE NIGHT HE WAS BETRAYED' PRAYED FOR HIS MISSION AND HIS FOLLOWERS

Waiting for some significant event can be a test of our patience and resolve. Our emotions will of course vary according to what it is we await. To prepare for a happy event like a wedding or a special birthday or an anniversary or a baby's birth is exciting and joyous. But if we anticipate a difficult confrontation or major illness or the death of a loved one, our waiting can be a time of anxiety and sadness. Our commitment and our character are often tested by how we face the big challenges of life.

What about the greatest test of all? Suppose you knew that tomorrow—or one day soon—your life would be ended and you were trying to sum up for someone what your life meant. What would you say?

In these chapters (13 to 17) we see Jesus facing a huge moment and answering that question. He had known that this crisis was inevitable. As John puts it: 'Jesus knew that his hour had come to depart from this world and go to the Father' (13:1). How did he react when the horror of the cross loomed ahead of him? He acted then as he had always done—he prayed to his 'Father in heaven'—just as he had taught his followers to do. That startling sense of intimacy between Jesus and the Father is where Jesus begins. Six times he says 'Father—Holy Father (17:11)' and 'Good Father' (17:25). So we too are invited to pray to such a loving, holy and good Father.

This was the night of his betrayal. Jesus was in the upper room with his disciples. He led them in a simple meal made memorable because of his words and actions. He talked simply, lovingly, movingly—clearly Jesus was leaving them and despite what he said their hearts *were* 'troubled' (14:1).

Then he prayed. Out loud, for John specifically tells us: 'He said' (17:1). The others held their breath. How could anyone capture the urgent and passionate tone of Jesus' prayer to his heavenly Father?

John was there. He did not have any of our modern recording methods, nor even a pen and papyrus. Yet he recalled this prayer—not the exact words but the way in which it showed how close Jesus was to his Father and how much Jesus loved them. It was a prayer, but it was also a farewell, a commitment, a plea, a commissioning, and a revelation. John knew that if he were to be true to Jesus and his presence with them then this prayer had to be recalled in his gospel. So it was woven into the beautiful portrait that he and his community created of Jesus' life and teaching.

In John 17 we have what William Temple described as 'perhaps the most sacred passage even in the four Gospels—the record of the Lord's prayer of self-dedication as it lived in the memory and imagination of His most intimate friend'.[1] So we tread on holy ground as we read this prayer. 'The prayer hangs between earth and heaven, between the pre- and post-resurrection moments of the Saviour's sojourn. It is presented as a prayer of the historical Jesus, but not confined to that; it is a prayer of the glorified Christ, but not discontinuous with Jesus of Nazareth.'[2]

So much is different from our day. However, as we read these words and open our hearts and minds can we not sense that these realities are unchanged? It is not a preacher's fantasy to suggest that we modern disciples are included in the sweep of this prayer. After all, John wrote his gospel for people who, like us, had never seen the earthly Jesus and hoped that they too were a part of this grand mission of God in our world.

So we are included and encouraged as we read that Jesus prayed: 'I ask also on behalf of those who will believe in me through their [the disciples'] words' (17:20).

The link between God, Jesus, the apostles and the church these centuries later is unbroken. The church is not an orphan in the world, a thing dislodged, a progeny of uncertain parentage, an accident of history, the frightened child of huddled rumours and superstitions. The pedigree of truth (as though truth needed to show its credentials) is beyond question: from God to Christ to the apostles to the church.[3]

There is a clear movement in three focal points, like three concentric circles, in the prayer. In the first section (17:1–5) Jesus prays for himself. The key word here is 'glory.' Jesus is about 'to enter the luminous realm of the Father's glory'.[4] John uses the word 'glory' eighteen times and 'glorify' twenty-three times in this chapter. In the second section (17:6–19), he prays for his disciples. The key word is 'kept'. Jesus asks the Father to preserve his disciples. In the third section (17:20–26), Jesus prays for the church. The key word is 'one'. Jesus desires his church to be united.

JESUS IN JOHN IS NO HAPLESS VICTIM BUT ONE WHO KNOWS WHEN HIS HOUR HAS COME

John encourages us to see that the glory of God is seen most of all in the 'hour' of sacrifice by Jesus. This 'hour' has been anticipated repeatedly (2:4; 7:6, 8, 30; 8:20; 12:27–28, 32–33). This 'hour of glory' is the reason why Jesus came to earth. Campbell Morgan once suggested that just as many Christians love to sing the hymn 'In the cross of Christ I glory', this was also 'the mind of Jesus himself as he went to it'.[5]

Whilst Jesus' 'hour' was unique and revelatory, we too are always coming to significant 'hours' in our lives. Both in minor and major ways we come to the place where we must say, as Jesus did, 'Father, the hour has come, the hour where I must make a choice as to whether I shall hold my life for myself, or whether I shall fling it away, and lay hold of the hope and the glory that lies beyond it'.

These hours are always coming to us. We call them disappointments or setbacks or tragedies, perhaps. We think of them as invasions of our privacy, attacking our right to live our own lives. But if we see them as Jesus saw them, we will recognise that each moment like this is an hour of great possibility.

Speaking of himself as *Son* (not 'me' or 'I') indicates, as clearly as we might want, the eternal relationship between the Father and Jesus. 'Son' means that he is God come to earth, and Father and Son are in absolute harmony in this great mission to save the world. We have a clear reference to the pre-existence of Jesus (17:5; see also 1:1, 2). As Paul expressed that coming to earth in Philippians: 'He emptied himself' (2:7).

Jesus rebukes our self-centred living. How can we talk about living 'for the glory of God' while our own lives are still filled with so much self-centredness and selfishness? CT Studd, an English test cricketer—an inspiration for some of us in our younger days—gave away his fortune and went out into the heart of Africa. He memorably declared: 'If Jesus Christ be God and died for me, then there is no sacrifice too great for me to make for him'.

How different this is from the prayers we usually pray for ourselves. Yes, we are encouraged to pray for ourselves: our problems, health, social and vocational issues, for forgiveness, for growth in holy living. But here we see Jesus' focus is that God will be fully known and glorified in all he does. Are we willing and longing that God's glory will be shown in us?

So John tells us that on the bloody tree Jesus was able to exclaim with his dying breath: 'It is finished!' (19:30). What was finished? The work that he had been given.

Why was this necessary? Here John offers us a clear answer: so that we might have eternal life! *Eternal life then is a gift.* And what is this? It is not a matter of going to heaven when we die and sitting around playing our harps. Whilst 'eternal' does speak of an endless existence, the principal emphasis is on the quality of the experience, the quality that is here and now. As WH Auden wrote: 'Eternity is the decision *now*, action *now*, one's neighbour *here*.⁶ It is to know the only true God and to know that Jesus Christ was sent by the Father and is the way to the Father (14:6). As John testifies in his gospel: 'We saw his true glory, the glory of the only Son of the Father' (1:14). John has told us again and again, that this is precisely what the coming of Jesus means. Read again those familiar words of John 3:16!

JESUS PRAYS FOR HIS DISCIPLES (AND US TOO!) AND VALUES THEM (AND US) AS A GIFT FROM THE FATHER

Again and again Jesus speaks of those whom the Father has given him (17:2; 6, 9, 24). The Father gives them to the Son and the Son gives them eternal life! He is grateful because these followers are a special gift from the Father. Those disciples, as we know only too well from our reading of the gospels, were a pretty feckless lot. They were unreliable and, in one notorious case, actually betrayed him for money. They looked an unpromising group. As do most of us!

But do you not sense that Jesus saw them in a different light? They are a source of pride and joy, a source of gratitude. He speaks of them (and us) as a gift from his Father (17:6, 9, 11, 24). The disciples are understood to be 'a gifted circle enfolded into the communication of the Father and the Son'.⁷ As AJ Gossip memorably expressed it: 'We speak of him as God's unspeakable gift to us. Christ on his side, incredibly enough, seems to regard us as an amazing gift from God to him'.

So they were special. Why? Because they were so talented and reliable? Scarcely, any more than we are! They were special because they belonged to both the Father and the Son. They share not only in that relationship, but also the task which the Father gave the Son—they are sent as the Son was sent (17:18; 20:21). That alone is what makes us special.

How do you feel about being described as a gift from God the Father to God the Son? It sounds rather impersonal, like so many presents to be handed out. But we are never regarded as mindless robots! Read again 17:6–8: these believers hear, obey, accept. What do they hear and obey and accept? That God is love, as shown in Jesus, the Son of God, sent from the heart of the Father, the most precious Word of life (17:7–8). That is still the essence of what we are called on to accept.

So what does Jesus ask God *for us*? Three things.

First, *unity*: I pray 'that they may all be one. As you, Father, are in me and I am in you, may they also be in us' (17:21). Jesus asks God that we, his later disciples, may be together, with a unity that is like the unity that exists between himself and God. And what is that? Jesus calls God 'Father', and he himself is named by God as 'my beloved Son'. Jesus' prayer for us is that we might be drawn into the primary relationship that characterises his own belonging to God; in other words, he asks that we might become sons and daughters of God.

The unity for which Jesus asks, then, is not based on who we are, but on who God is. The unity for which Jesus prays is not dependent upon our ability to overcome division, but upon God's constant love for us in spite of that division. Jesus is not praying for some uniform expression of faith, in which all believe the same things without variance. The 'unity' here is not the absence of our disagreements. Slowly—with God's help—we come to see others through the eyes of Jesus Christ.

Some have sought to establish special communities of faith. Dietrich Bonhoeffer wrote in his classic study *Life Together* about the problems that this form of intentional community can experience:

> Innumerable times a whole Christian community has broken down because it had sprung from a wish dream. The serious Christian, set down for the first time in a Christian community, is likely to bring with him a very definite idea of what Christian life together should be and try to realize it. But God's grace speedily shatters such dreams. Just as surely as God desires to lead us to a knowledge of genuine Christian fellowship, so surely must we be overwhelmed by a great disillusionment with others, with Christians in general, and if we are fortunate, with ourselves … He who loves his dream of a community more than the Christian community itself becomes the destroyer of the latter, even though his personal intentions may be ever so honest and earnest and sacrificial.[8]

Second, Jesus asks that we might have a deep sense of *presence*: 'Father, I desire that those also, whom you have given me, may be *with me* where I am, to see my glory, which you have given me ...' (17:24, italics added). Jesus prays that we will live in his presence and share his glory. This is not a prayer that we might know more historical facts about Jesus. His prayer is not that we might know *about* him, but that we might be *with* him and have a *share* in his living glory.

And what is that? 'Glory' in scripture—and especially in the Gospel of John—is the manifestation of God's being and nature in a way that is accessible to human experience. God's life, and all it entails—truth, light, grace, mercy, justice—are given to Jesus, according to this prayer, from 'the foundation of the earth' (17:24). That *is* his glory. And he prays that we have a share in that manifestation of God's presence.

Third, Jesus prays that we may dwell in love—the love of God—'that the love with which you have loved me may be in them' (17:26). This is the most profound of the requests. The same love which is God's own, the love which defines the nature of God from the foundation of the earth, the love between the Father and the Son, that love—Jesus asks—may be in us.

The really stunning thing about this prayer is *what it says about God*. You see when *Jesus* prays, it is not just the same as when you and I pray. We come to God as God's creatures and say—as creature to our creator—'our Father in heaven'. But Jesus, in John's theology, is himself one with God. Jesus is the Word of God that became flesh and dwelt amongst us. *God with us. God for us. God beside us.*

Thus, when Jesus prays it is a conversation in the heart of God. This prayer is God the Word addressing God the Father in the power of God the Holy Spirit. In other words, this prayer is a window into the dynamic life of the God who is trinity, Father, Son and Spirit. Jesus prays that we, as individuals and as the church, will be drawn into the trinitarian life of God. Nothing less than that.

So we read: 'to those who received him, who believed in his name, he gave power to become *children of God*' (John 1:12). When the risen Jesus met Mary Magdalene, he commissioned her: 'Go to my brothers and say to them, "I am ascending to my Father and your Father, to my God and your God".' *My* Father and *your* Father. In the resurrection, the relationship that the Son and Father have always shared now extends to those for whom he prayed before his death.

Here, surely, we may also find a clear vision of what our calling and mission should be. Jesus is concerned about us living in the world. Note that the word 'world' is used here twelve times! While John's gospel memorably portrays God's love for the world of people (3:16) as the basis for Christ's coming, it also sees grave dangers for believers in the value systems of the world. The 'world' here does not mean the created world that inspires with its beauty but can also terrify us with its fury. John uses the word to describe society organised against God, in opposition to God. That is the origin of all disciples, including us—we were in that world. That is where we were before Jesus came to bring us true life. Whilst we remain in this hostile environment we belong to a different order of reality. Light in darkness is how John thinks of it.

One response to such dangers presented by the world is for Christians to live in a world of their own—to withdraw from society's challenges and human needs. The greater danger for most today is probably the opposite—not withdrawal from the world but conformity with its prevailing values and politics.

Many of us tend to repeat the simple mantra: '*In* the world but not *of* the world'. But this conceals complex and subtle challenges: How are we meant to relate to our prevailing culture? Jesus didn't ask God to protect us from evil or to protect us from bad things happening. We are called to be in the real world, where we have cancer, car crashes, tsunamis, earthquakes, terrorists, economic crises, wars, and homeless children, but not to be of the world in the way we try to make sense of it. That is why the cross is always central to our understanding of what God is doing in our world.

Neither isolation, nor assimilation, but mission is the vision of Jesus for us. Teresa of Avila is commonly (but wrongly, it seems) quoted as saying: 'Christ has no body on earth but yours, no hands but yours, no feet but yours; yours are the eyes through which the compassion of Christ looks out on a hurting world, yours are the feet with which he goes about doing good; yours are the hands with which he is to bless now'.[9]

Jesus still prays to the Father to take care of each one of his followers, to protect them from evil, to perfect them in goodness, to promote their growth in grace and unity. The Irish blessing summarises exactly the meaning of this prayer: 'Until we meet again, may God hold you all in the palm of his hand'.

Questions for discussion

1. Discuss the feelings that you have when someone assures you that they are praying for you. Is it always helpful to tell others we are doing this?

2. Why do you think that this prayer has (most probably since the 17th century) been spoken of as 'the high-priestly prayer' of Jesus? How helpful an idea is this? Whilst we often discuss the pre-existence of Jesus, should we not also emphasise the 'post-existence' of Jesus? (Look at Romans 8:34, Hebrews 4:15, 5:7–9, 10:19–22 for help in this question.)

3. JS Stewart has observed: 'The praying Christ is the supreme argument for prayer'. In what ways should the example of Jesus shape our attitude to prayer? Discuss significant times in his life when we are told that Jesus prayed.

4. Explore the issues about how we have this prayer of Jesus preserved when no one was there to write it down. Does this help us understand the creation of this whole gospel?

5. Can you identify any parallels between this prayer and the Lord's Prayer?

6. Suggest ways in which this prayer of Jesus for himself and his mission could help us as we pray for ourselves.

7. Look closely at the times in which Jesus spoke about his 'hour' in John's gospel (2:4; 7:6, 8, 30; 8:20; 12:27–28, 32–33.). What does this tell us about the theology of the cross in this gospel?

8. Look closely at the quotation from Bonhoeffer in this study and discuss its relevance for you and your community of faith. In what ways should we seek to promote the unity of the church?

9. As you look over this long chapter, what are the main points that have impressed you and how will these have an impact on your life as a believer?

Further along the way

1. W Temple, *Readings in St John's Gospel* (London: Macmillan, 1961), p. 293.

2. FB Craddock, *John* (Atlanta: John Knox Press, 1982), p. 123.

3. Craddock, *John*, p. 126.

4. AJ Kelly and FJ Moloney, *Experiencing God in the Gospel of John* (New York: Paulist Press, 2003), p. 333.

5. GC Morgan *The Four Gospels* (London: Oliphants, 1956), p. 271.

6. WH Auden, as quoted by T Winton, *The Boy Behind the Curtain* (Melbourne: Hamish Hamilton, 2016), p. 115.

7. Kelly and Moloney, *Experiencing God*, p. 338.

8. D Bonhoeffer, *Life Together* (London: SCM Press, 1954), pp. 15–16.

9. These lines are in common use but evidently do not appear in any of the works of Teresa. http://mimuspolyglottos.blogspot.com/2011/11/whose-hands-another-possible-case-of.html accessed 28/11/16

'Crucifixion with a donor', Hieronymus Bosch, c. 1490

CHAPTER TEN

HERE IS YOUR MOTHER: JESUS AND MARY
(JOHN 19:25–27)

> In paintings and poetry, with song and sculpture, from rarefied theological ruminations to the most vulgar piety, women and men have pondered the mystery of Mary, the mother of Jesus of Nazareth. Twenty centuries of Christian history have witnessed an astonishing variety of expressions to the church's fascination with this woman.[1]

For innumerable Christians, Mary still occupies a central place in their devotional life. The 'Hail Mary' is a characteristic form of prayer for Roman Catholic believers. Some extraordinary reports of appearances by Mary—often accompanied by miracles—are also a feature of Marian veneration in many places. Yet at the same time some of these more extreme practices and the worship of Mary as the 'Mother of God' or even as 'Co-Mediator' (with Christ) have alienated Protestants since the sixteenth century. Subsequently, many Protestants only think of Mary in negative terms, insisting only on what they do not believe about her.

This is an understandable if regrettable response. Whilst reformers like Luther had a deep respect for Mary, any beliefs or practices judged to be contrary to Scripture were rejected. Some reactions were extreme. One of the more famous is the story about John Knox, the reformer in Scotland. In his early life he was taken as a prisoner on the French galleys and on one occasion the Catholic chaplain on the ship held up a painted wooden statue of the Blessed Virgin Mary and encouraged the prisoners to genuflect and show respect. When the statue was forcibly placed in Knox's hands he grabbed it and threw it overboard. 'Let our lady now save herself', he said. 'She is light enough; let her learn to swim!'[2]

In more recent times such anti-Marian extremes have been modified, but Protestants generally and evangelicals in particular still have difficulties with some Roman dogma, especially the teaching on Mary's immaculate conception, the perpetual virginity of Mary and the assumption of Mary (that Mary, body and soul, went to heaven without dying). Generally Mary is accepted as *Theotokos* ('God Bearer', or, as Jaroslav Pelikan suggests, 'the one who gave birth to the one who is God') as defined at the Council of Ephesus in 431 CE amidst divisive debates.[3] Evangelicals especially maintain a strong belief in the virgin birth. The insistence that Christ is the only mediator and that the Bible is the supreme authority for theology—especially Christology—has been determinative for Protestants. Mary's selection for her unique role as mother of Jesus was solely a matter of grace and not due to any unique merit by her. On the other hand, much contemporary biblical work on Mary by Roman Catholic scholars has been illuminating and constructive.

Few would today disagree with the view that Protestants should cease to be merely negative and neglect Mary, but rather should rediscover her as a devout and special believer who played a unique role in the story of Jesus.

MARY IN THE GOSPELS

There is much about Mary in the New Testament, but very little in John. He has none of the 'big' stories about Mary found only in Matthew and Luke, such as the visitation by the angel Gabriel, the salutation by Elizabeth, the virgin birth, the birth stories, the flight to Egypt and the twelve-year old Jesus visiting the temple in Jerusalem. Important as these patently are for a full understanding of Mary in the New Testament, we are not here concerned with these stories. Presumably the author knew them but seems to have had no interest in them, either because they were well known to his community or—more likely—because he had a quite different aspect of Mary's role to reveal.

As we are examining encounters with Jesus in John's gospel, we come to reflect on this most intimate and unique 'encounter'. It seems unusual to speak about the relationship between a mother and son as an encounter but here we are invited to consider Mary simply as this gospel depicts her.

Two striking features in John may be noted. First, she is never called Mary but simply 'the mother of Jesus'. Second, she is only mentioned on two occasions: the miracle at Cana (John 2:1–11) and standing beneath the cross (John 19:25–27). In both scenes Jesus addressed her as 'Woman', and in each case there is specific reference to the 'hour of Jesus'. John invites readers to think of her as a 'woman' disciple whose story is linked with the hour of Jesus, which readers of the gospel know is his hour of exaltation—on the cross. There is one reference to the fact that people knew both Jesus' father and mother (6:42), and in 8:41 there is a hint that there were rumours about the illegitimacy of Jesus' birth.

Because there are only these two stories in which Mary is present and, given the emphasis on symbolism in John, scholars have generally taken one of two positions. Some have thought of her as a symbol—of the church, or the new Eve, or Jewish Christianity, or something else! Others have regarded her role as more straightforward, as a 'functionary' to advance the story: her presence prompts the miracle at Cana, and at the cross her presence reveals Jesus' filial affection, his concern to fulfil his role as carer for his mother. At the same time, of course, Mary stands as an example of true faith.

We will seek to be guided by our concern to discover how these stories develop our understanding of who Jesus is, and how we today may be helped as followers of Jesus.

MARY AT CANA (JOHN 2:1–12)

This story is deeply significant in John as it marks the first sign to reveal Jesus' glory and to initiate faith in his disciples (2:11).[4] There are hints of what lies ahead, most especially in Jesus' reply to his mother that his hour had not yet come (2:4).

The story introduces his mother before Jesus plays any part in the event. Her maternal role is the central aspect of her character, as in some Eastern customs where a woman is honoured by being known only as the mother of a son. Mary's identity in John is established solely by reference to her son. Her role is simply to report to Jesus that the wine has all gone. That she turned to her son and not her husband, as would otherwise have been the norm, implies that she was a widow. Of course, she also must have known of the unique character of her son. There is no request, simply the report to him.

What Jesus said in response to Mary has puzzled readers. First, he addressed her as 'Woman' which sounds to us a somewhat remote or even rude way for a son to speak to his mother. This is also the way Jesus addressed her from the cross, and this suggests that this manner of address was not as unfeeling as we might be tempted to think. Scholars claim that this way of speaking was not without precedent and does not denote any disrespect. Most probably the use of the word 'Woman' in John suggests a symbolic role for Mary, as already suggested.

More difficult is the precise meaning of what Jesus said to this 'woman' (2:4). If we look at different translations this will become evident. In the Greek, it reads as: 'Jesus said: "What is to me and to you, woman?"' which explains why translators have a problem. It suggests a rebuke, and this is followed by the insistence that his hour had not yet come. This story is thus linked with the saying to Mary at the cross that brings to an end his fulfilment of his hour: 'It is finished!' (19:30). Jesus was asserting that his destiny would move far beyond domestic anxieties about weddings and wine, and he was beginning to follow the path that would lead to this final hour.

In any case, Jesus' words seem to be a refusal to do what his mother implicitly has asked him to do. The difficulty with this interpretation is, of course, that Jesus *does* respond to his mother in a way that is theologically significant; his sign shows the super-abundance of life that will come through him. The story is not offering us clues about catering at a humble Galilean wedding but rather clues about the bringer of abundant divine gifts.

Mary's role as a determined mother is expanded to show her faith in Jesus when she commanded the attendants to do whatever Jesus tells them, thus serving as a model for all disciples. She had set in motion the occasion for the first sign. After the miracle, Mary, the family and the disciples spend time in Capernaum—with much to talk about (2:12)!

MARY AT THE CROSS (JOHN 19:25–27)

This is a beautiful but theologically profound scene. Once again Mary is simply described as the mother of Jesus, and is standing beneath the cross with three other women, one of whom is Mary Magdalene (whom we discuss in the next chapter). The other women are named, but the only man present, as with Mary, is not named. She does not speak, but is near enough to hear what Jesus said. This is an intensely emotional scene. At the very least, the words of Jesus suggest a filial concern for his mother. He does not want to die without securing protection for her.

The raw human emotion of the scene is gripping. James Denney wrote: 'From the pulpit of his cross Jesus preached a sermon on the fifth commandment' about honouring parents.[5] William Barclay highlights the emotion of the event:

> There is something infinitely moving in the fact that Jesus in the agony of the cross, in the moment when the salvation of the world hung in balance, thought of the loneliness of his mother in the days when he was taken away. Jesus never forgot the duties that lay to his hand. He was Mary's eldest son, and even in the moment of his cosmic battle, he never forgot the simple things that lay near home. To the end of the day, even on the cross, Jesus was thinking more of the sorrows of others than his own.[6]

Beverly Gaventa is surely correct in seeing this event as completing Jesus' separation from all that belongs to his earthly life. Just as he is stripped of his clothing, he 'divests' himself of his mother and of the beloved disciple.[7] The human family, with whom he shares early in the gospel, is removed at the 'hour' of his return to the Father.

Roman Catholics have tended to concentrate on what these words mean for Mary, whilst Protestants have tended to focus on what was said to the male disciple. But efforts to elevate one or the other are misguided, since it is through her relationship with the disciple that Mary contributes to the establishment of the family of God.[8]

The sacred words have echoed across the centuries: 'Woman, behold your son' and 'Behold your mother'. Mary learnt that she was to be a mother as a disciple, not a mother and also a disciple.[9] Witherington suggests that John portrays Mary and the beloved disciple as 'archetypal disciples, male and female, standing together beneath the cross as examples to all'.[10] In this sense she became a model woman who obeyed her Lord's direction. Her example is as a model of a disciple on the journey of faith.

The formula 'Behold …' has been used before in this gospel: 'Behold the lamb of God who takes away the sin of the world' (1:29 and 36); 'Behold, this one baptizes and everyone comes to him' (3:26); and then by Pilate: 'Behold your king' (19:14). Clearly, 'Behold' suggests that an important or unusual event is at hand.

John seems to say that the disciple immediately ('from that hour') led Mary away to his own home so that she would be spared the horror of watching the actual death of her son (19:27). As John expressed it: 'After this, Jesus knew that all was finished' (19:28). In any case, as far as the story in John goes, Mary does not appear again, and Jesus has no mother. Luke reports that Mary and the brothers of Jesus were later with the other disciples in Jerusalem (Acts 1:14).

A natural conclusion has been drawn from these verses that Mary became the mother of all believers—a new family came into being, 'born not of the will of man but of God' (1:12). Newbigin has wisely commented that 'even a very understandable reaction against a deformed Mariology must not be allowed to exclude the recognition of the place of Mary which has been and is so important a part of Christian piety from the beginning'.[11]

Her challenge to us is to question whether we are as ready to love and serve Jesus as she was. This challenge is real because the emphasis on her life in the gospel is not that she was the mother of Jesus—though we honour her for that unique role—but because she became a loyal and loving disciple of the Jesus whom she came to love, not as an earthly son but as the living Son of God. Her experience was painful but remains a shining example for us. Can we emulate her in this faith?

Questions for discussion

1. What are the main impressions that you have about Mary from the New Testament stories about her? Are there any special ways in which her story has influenced you in your faith and spirituality?

2. Read the summary of how Mary has been interpreted across the history of the church. Why do you think there has been so much tension between Roman Catholics and Protestants about this? What harm has this tension done to Christian relations between denominations? Are there any local conversations in which you might share with Roman Catholic believers?

3. Read carefully the story about the miracle at Cana (John 2). What do you see as important about the role of Mary in this story?

4. Read John 19:25–27. Try to describe how Mary must have felt. What do you think are the most important issues that this story develops?

5. In what sense do you understand Mary to be an example of faith in John's gospel?

1. BR Gaventa, *Mary. Glimpses of the Mother of Jesus* (Minneapolis: Fortress Press, 1999), p. 1.

2. T George, 'The Blessed Virgin Mary in Evangelical Perspective', in *Mary Mother of God* (CE Braaten and RW Jenson [eds], Grand Rapids: Eerdmans, 2004), pp. 100–101.

3. J Pelikan, *Mary Through the Centuries* (New Haven: Yale University Press, 1996), p. 55.

4. For a further reflection on this story, see my *On the Way to Faith*, pp. 12–20.

5. J Denney, as cited by FD Bruner, *The Gospel of John: A Commentary* (Grand Rapids: Eerdmans, 2012), p. 1108.

6. W Barclay, *The Gospel of John* (Vol 2, Edinburgh: Saint Andrew Press, 1957), p. 299.

7. Gaventa, *Mary*, p. 91.

8. CM Conway, *Men and Women in the Fourth Gospel. Gender and Johannine Characterization* (Atlanta: Society of Biblical Literature, 1999), p. 82.

9. B Witherington III, *Women in the Ministry of Jesus* (Cambridge: Cambridge University Press, 1984), p. 95.

10. B Witherington III, *Women in the Earliest Churches* (Cambridge: Cambridge University Press, 1988), p. 175.

11. L Newbigin, *The Light Has Come* (Grand Rapids: Eerdmans, 1982), p. 255.

'Noli Me Tangere', Musée du Petit Palais, c. 1400

CHAPTER ELEVEN

I HAVE SEEN THE LORD: JESUS AND MARY MAGDALENE
(JOHN 20:1–18)

Mary Magdalene! The name has resounded across the centuries. Yet the gospels tell us very little about her; and so much of what has been written is confused and fictional: 'a mix of lust, loyalty, belief and prostitution'.[1] The gospel texts are all too often read through the lens of bizarre legends embodied in numerous works of art and fiction. Why has this been so?

More particularly, what precisely is this woman's role in the gospels? Sadly, all the myths and bizarre inventions have obscured her unique role in the early church as an 'apostle to the apostles'.

There is, therefore, a double challenge for believers today: first to expose the myths and then to focus on the gospel records. This woman's unique story of encounters with Jesus in John offers us an enduring paradigm of the journey towards faith.

MARY MAGDALENE: THE MAKING OF MANY MYTHS

The New Testament tells us only a few brief facts about this Mary. She had 'seven devils' cast out of her by Jesus and she became a follower. She stood with other women at the cross, discovered the empty tomb and was later spoken to by the risen Christ who told her to tell the other disciples. That is all there is—highly significant certainly, but nothing more.

After the New Testament era, Mary Magdalene played a prominent role in several Gnostic texts as a mediator of revelation or in conversation between the risen Christ and his disciples. The rediscovered text of the 'Gospel of Mary' has received extensive study in recent years.[2] The other problem, within the orthodox mainstream of interpretation, was that other gospel stories were conflated (or 'contaminated') with those that specify her. Sexism and misogyny have been claimed as the reason for this.[3] Western tradition, certainly by the time of Gregory the Great in the sixth century, identified her with the 'woman who was a sinner' and anointed Christ's feet in Simon's house (Luke 7:37). She was also claimed to be Mary the sister of Martha who also anointed him (John 12:3). The gospels give no support to this conflation of quite distinct stories.

Some insist that the emphasis on her sexuality has suppressed her testimony. Susan Hoskins concluded:

> And so the transformation of Mary Magadalen was complete. From the gospel figure with her active role as herald of the New Life—the Apostle before the Apostles—she became the reformed whore and Christianity's model of repentance: a manageable, controllable figure, an effective weapon and instrument of propaganda against her own sex.[4]

Again in the West, a very popular but quite unfounded legend had arisen by the ninth century that this Mary, with Martha and Lazarus, came to the south of France by sea; in the Middle Ages her supposed relics were venerated at various places in Provence. She became the patron saint of the cosmetic industry in the Middle Ages.

Some extraordinary works of art from the fourteenth century featuring Mary Magdalene provide dramatic symbols of conversion from great sinfulness. She was honoured as the great penitent, the sexual sinner who was capable of great love. Mary was a counterpoint to the sinless Virgin Mary in fourteenth century piety.[5] Jane Schaberg summarises the way in which she has been depicted in art:

> Sometimes she is hideous, anorexic and haunted, more often beautiful, sensual. Almost always through the thirteenth to the nineteenth century she is nude or partially nude. The exposed breast alone is a complex symbol, often signaling the Magdalene's seductiveness, a pathological sexual interest lurking in the background of her sanctity, her love of God; her inability to attain a pure, disinterested contemplation. An object of legitimized voyeurism, Mary Magdalene's eroticism could express pious emotionalism, or pious pornography …[6]

It seems that the modern era has even outdone the medieval years for incredible imaginings about her in art, novels and plays. *Jesus Christ Superstar* gave prominence to the Magdalene in which she sings—as did Judas—'I don't know how to love him'. The combination of the demonic and the erotic has proved to be irresistible.

Some contemporary biblical scholars have also entered into the realm of speculation. One suggestion, for example, was that Mary was the bride at the wedding of Cana and that after the miracle of the water into wine, her betrothed (who was John) left her to follow Jesus! John Shelby Spong thus joins an ancient line of interpreters who have speculated that Mary was the wife or the lover of Jesus. Barbara Thiering asserted from her fantastic conflations of New Testament and Dead Sea scrolls that Mary was married to Jesus and had three children![7] A sensationalist 'history' titled *Holy Blood, Holy Grail* (1982) was succeeded by Dan Brown's bestseller *The Da Vinci Code* (2003), which takes these legends to a fantastic level!

Enough! These layers of complex additions across 1500 years need to be stripped away and the true story revealed, because that is itself sufficient mystery and authentic inspiration! Mary Magdalene needs to be remembered for her role as a female disciple who became the apostle to the apostles.

MARY MAGDALENE IN THE NEW TESTAMENT

THE HEALING OF MARY FROM MAGDALA

We are not given a precise account of Mary becoming a disciple of Jesus. Her first mention is in Luke 8:2–3 where she is named first among a group of 'some women' who were travelling with Jesus and the twelve. There she is—'Mary, called Magdalene, from whom seven demons had gone out'—a brief but intriguing introduction. 'Magdalene' means that she came from Magdala, a prosperous trading centre usually identified with the site of Migdal on the western shore of the Sea of Galilee about five kilometres north of Tiberias.

Unlike other male disciples who are named in a family connection, nothing is known about this Mary's family—nothing about a father or a brother or a sister; she is known only by her hometown. Like the other women in the gospels, there is no story of her call to discipleship and no detailed story about her healing. Yet patently she came to be a follower of Jesus after he had cast out seven demons from her (Luke 8:2, Mark 16:9). What illnesses, confusions, sadnesses and tragedies that brief reference to seven demons conceals! Perhaps we would today say that she suffered from a severe mental illness, perhaps manic depression. Why seven? Possibly, it has been suggested, because Jesus exorcised her repeatedly.[8] The joyous outcome was that she was set free; she joined with Joanna and Susanna in helping to fund the Galilean movement, and helped in a practical way by providing food for the group.

This reference in Luke is an isolated and intriguing insight into this small group of women who itinerated with Jesus and the twelve. (See also Matthew 27:55–56.) 'To follow Jesus meant travelling around, leaving everything behind and following him. It meant living in poverty and simplicity which one had chosen for oneself. It meant having dealings with the other disciples, rich and poor, from the city or the country, whether zealot, toll collector or fisherman.'[9] Such public travelling-together of mixed genders would have been offensive to Jewish sentiments. There is, however, no recorded hint of criticism about Jesus on this score, and de Boer comments that 'a veil of mystery hangs over the women'.[10]

This reminds us of the remarkable way in which Jesus welcomed and affirmed women. This is worth celebrating in itself. Long before the rise of the modern feminist movement, Dorothy Sayers wrote:

> (Woman) had never known a man like this Man—there never has been such another. A prophet and teacher who never nagged at them, never flattered or coaxed or patronized; who never made arch jokes about them … who rebuked without querulousness and praised without condescension … who never mapped out their sphere for them, never urged them to be feminine or jeered at them for being female; who had no axe to grind and no uneasy male dignity to defend, who took them as he found them and was completely unself-conscious. There is no act, no sermon, no parable in the whole Gospel that borrows its pungency from female perversity; nobody could possibly guess from the words and deeds of Jesus that there was anything 'funny' about woman's nature.[11]

Mary moved from no faith to faith because with her profound needs she had encountered Jesus and been healed.

BENEATH THE CROSS OF JESUS (JOHN 19:25)

John first mentions Mary Magdalene—without any other comment—as he tells the story of the cross. Presumably the traditions about her (as in the other gospels) were well known. Let us not forget that the male disciples, apart from 'the disciple whom he loved', seem to have been absent from that tragic scene. Women play significant roles in John, sometimes shaming the male disciples, as with Mary's anointing compared with Judas. Here at the cross, the courage of these women suggests how genuine disciples should act.

Mary Magdalene, along with Mary (the mother of Jesus), her sister (presumably Salome, the aunt of Jesus in Mark 15:40, the mother of the sons of Zebedee in Matthew 27:56), and another Mary (the wife of Clopas) were there.[12] These four women stand over against the four soldiers, who were arguing over the bloodstained woven clothes that the women had perhaps supplied. Despite the criticism of some scholars that the Romans would not have allowed relatives and friends to be so close to the scene of a public execution, there are recorded precedents and the tradition is unanimous that these women were there, on that day, in that place. They saw it all. They were faithful and loyal disciples. Jesus was able to gasp out that his mother was now the mother of the disciple and she was to be his mother. Mary from Magdala heard this too.

Who can fully imagine Mary's heartache and distress, standing beneath that cross? A Victorian Scottish woman, Elizabeth Clephane, wrote a much-loved hymn inspired by the women who stood there: 'Beneath the cross of Jesus I fain would take my stand'. One stanza captures the meaning of what Mary saw there—beneath that cross—for believers today:

> Upon that cross of Jesus
> Mine eyes at times can see
> The very dying form of One
> Who suffered there for me;
> And from my smitten heart with tears
> Two wonders I confess—
> The wonders of his glorious love,
> And my own worthlessness.

That Mary saw at first hand the suffering and death of her loved teacher meant that she was as astonished as anyone when she had a life-changing encounter with the risen Jesus.

FINDING AN EMPTY TOMB (JOHN 20:1–10)

John tells us that Mary went alone to the tomb, early on the Sunday morning, while it was still dark. To be out alone in this way was unusual for a woman in this culture. The other gospels affirm that a number of women came, anxious about how the stone might be moved away from the entrance to the tomb. How to reconcile these two statements should not worry us since it is possible that John is focusing on the experience of this one disciple. When she saw the disciples, she reported that *we* do not know 'where they have laid him' (20:2).

What should not be minimised is the common affirmation that the tomb was empty. As JAT Robinson noted, no one expected to find a grave empty; nor would they have associated this with the resurrection, but with foul play.[13]

Peering through the half-light, Mary saw that the tomb was empty but did not look inside or wait around—she raced back to tell Peter and John ('the other disciple') who sprinted to the scene. Presumably Mary came panting along after them as Peter and John went right into the tomb. Peter saw the linen wrappings neatly placed together, thus removing a fear that tomb robbers had been there (and centuries later assuring one Tasmanian Baptist lady in 1901 that Jesus set us 'an example of tidiness in the way He left His grave clothes').[14] The other disciple gathered sufficient courage to enter himself and John tells us that 'he saw and believed' (20:8).

But what exactly did he believe? That the tomb was empty, certainly—but was this a belief in the resurrection? Evidently not, because John then adds the puzzling statement that they did not yet understand the scripture: 'that he must rise from the dead' (20:9). What scripture was meant? Suggestions include Hosea 6:2 or Jonah 1:17, but it became a matter of common faith that Jesus was raised 'on the third day according to the scriptures' (1 Cor. 15:4). That the disciples simply then went home (20:10) suggests that the beloved disciple believed that the tomb was indeed empty. As Minear has commented: 'Nowhere else in the New Testament is it suggested that faith in the risen Lord produced such indifference, as if nothing at all had happened to change things'.[15] The main point here is, of course, that the disciples still had far to go in their journey in faith—they discovered the resurrection truth by stages.

Mary stayed in the garden, all alone—or so she thought!

TALKING WITH ANGELS (JOHN 20:11–12)

Mary was still in the dark, not only physically but in her faith. She wept bitterly, grieving over the loss of her beloved Jesus. Drawn to the open tomb she at last brought herself to stoop down to look inside. John simply records that she saw two angels sitting there (present tense in the original to emphasise the sudden shock). One sat where the head of Jesus would have been and one was seated at the spot where his scarred feet would have been. He may have been crucified between two thieves, but he was buried in the tomb between two angels. Some Church Fathers wondered whether this was an allusion to the ancient propitiatory Mercy Seat with the cherubim on either side of the great sacrifice. His blood became a mercy seat (see Romans 3:25).[16]

The ensuing exchange is extraordinary. Mary does not seem unduly surprised that these 'angels in white'—probably a symbol of joy—were there. They are perhaps marking the site as holy, this place of resurrection. Perhaps she was by now so emotionally exhausted that nothing could surprise her, even seeing angels in the tomb. Peter and John had not seen angels there. After they asked why she was weeping, Mary replied with a simple cry from the heart: 'They have taken away my Lord, and I do not know where they have laid him'. There is her personal faith—'*my* Lord'—and bewilderment about mysterious persons—'they'—who have taken his body away. Could it have been Nicodemus, returned to complete the burial process? The soldiers? The Jewish leaders? She was still preoccupied with death and had no idea about the Life that was about to engage her. The angels made no response to her cry and had no further part to play in the story although perhaps they motioned to her to look behind her.

CLINGING TO THE PAST (JOHN 20:14-17)

She saw a figure, but in the half darkness and with tear-filled eyes she could not see exactly who was there; she naturally thought it was the gardener, who would have had a legitimate reason to be there. Perhaps he could tell her where the precious remains of Jesus had been taken. The 'gardener' asks her 'Why are you weeping?' but adds, 'Whom [not what] are you seeking?' She imagined that she could be strong enough to 'take him away'. Still with a heavy heart, she hoped that she might be given some further light on the whereabouts of Jesus. The irony of Mary asking the living Jesus for the body of her beloved should not be missed. It is a striking feature of resurrection stories that those who had known him had difficulty in recognising the risen Lord (Luke 24:1–35; John 21:1–8).

The simple word 'Mary' made her heart leap. She now turned and said to this figure, 'Rabbouni', a word which John wanted to keep in the original language because of its immediacy and as a sacred memory; it was a word, John tells us, which means 'teacher'—or it could have a personal indication: 'my dear rabbi'.[17] Nowhere in John's gospel is Jesus called by his given name. In much Hebrew literature 'Rabbouni' was the form of address used in prayer to God. Had not Jesus taught them to think of him as the good shepherd who knows the name of each sheep (John 10:3)? So now, Jesus finds her and speaks her name, just as he had so often spoken to her. Her persistence had been rewarded.

This single astonishing encounter is a dramatic story of recognition. How brilliantly it is told. As CH Dodd commented about this passage: 'It has something indefinably first-hand about it. It stands in any case. There is nothing quite like it in the Gospels. Is there anything quite like it in all ancient literature?'[18]

Fiorenza insists that this encounter should not be psychologised. Mary is not so much the 'great lover' of Jesus who is upset by his death but rather a representative of the disciples' situation after the departure of Jesus.[19] She is depicted as the faithful disciple who continues to 'seek Jesus' and is called by name. We may trace the progression in Mary's experience. In the darkness, she at first had no belief that Jesus was alive. Then she moved to the next stage, calling him 'Teacher'. Yet Mary had more to learn.

We must pause to emphasise the reality and wonder of the resurrection. A poem by Rowan Williams imagines Christ emerging from the tomb, 'death running off his limbs like drops from a shower'.[20] This story of Mary Magdalene should not only be read as a part of the Easter liturgy but also celebrated regularly as a reminder of the journey from unbelief to faith to which we all are called. The resurrection of Jesus is a core Christian belief to be celebrated with joy by all disciples. After the resurrection, no one need stand weeping without hope, as Mary once did, at the tomb of a loved one.

Peter Stiles has captured something of that first Resurrection Sunday:

> A glorious unveiling, lightning, presence,
>   a tearing, releasing, breathless running.
> News that exploded like soul searing fission,
>   for Jerusalem, Empire, Age, a tired Earth.
> But a touching, a healing, a balm like no other,
>   the bunting of grace in the shards of cruelty,
>   the banner of joy for the grimace of sadness.[21]

In what tone did Jesus say to her, 'Do not touch me ...' (20:17)? On a first reading, it can sound rather cold and rejecting—an unfeeling rebuke. Scholars, however, note that the tense of the command denotes that this was a continuing action: 'Do not keep on holding and touching me.' It is not that the resurrection body of Jesus had some strange 'otherly' quality. It was certainly not, as one scholar has proposed, that Jesus was naked, having been stripped of his grave clothes![22] Thomas was bidden to put his hands into the wounds of Jesus (John 20:27), and Matthew tells of women who clung to his feet (Mathew 28:9). Mary did not just poke a finger at Jesus but quite spontaneously embraced him, as doubtless she had often done out of love and gratitude. But now she hears: 'Do not cling to me'.

The theological significance of the encounter is important. She is called to move beyond the *naïveté* of a simple faith. He is not a dead Messiah. His voice is still near and familiar, but this is a new age. She must give up the old relationship, dependent as it was on where Jesus might have been physically. She must move from 'my Teacher' to 'my Lord'. This is a new relationship. The empty tomb and these words of Jesus are signs to lead Mary—and through her all the disciples—to this new reality of communion with Jesus, a communion unaffected by time or place. This is a different way of 'being in touch', as it were—a fuller and permanent union of disciple and Saviour.

Who could blame Mary for missing the old way? We often still do just that. Ben Witherington has suggested: 'many struggling churches cling to their past in a way that is neither healthful nor helpful'.[23] We older believers can all too easily long for what we recall as 'the good old days'. But—like Mary—we too are people of the resurrection. Whilst we may and must learn from the past, we cannot live in the past.

There is one final 'not yet' that Mary must hear: 'I have not yet ascended to the Father' (John 20:17). This has been called one of the hardest verses to interpret in the whole gospel, although it clearly means that Jesus is on his way, ascending to the Father. When we think of the ascension of Jesus we tend to think of the account in Acts 1:9–11, but this is John's version. Theologically, this verse is claiming that the cross, the resurrection and the ascension are all bound together in the mission of Jesus.

A MISSION TO THE APOSTLES: 'I HAVE SEEN THE LORD' (JOHN 20:18)

This saying of Jesus gave a special mission to Mary. She was directed to tell the disciples—and her message was brief but powerful —'I have seen the Lord'. She told them what Jesus had said to her. They were now a special family. They were the brothers and sisters of Jesus and they had a common Father: 'my Father and your Father'.

Mary Magdalene, then, had a special mission: she was the sent one (an apostle) to the apostles. Think about that for a moment. This woman, who had been battling seven demons which were destroying her life, was rescued by Jesus and became a devoted follower. After the horrors of seeing the cross, she has now seen the risen Lord and is the chosen one to announce this miracle to her male friends. How sad that this primal role of a witness has been overshadowed by all the mythical nonsense that was later attached to her name!

Thorwald Lorenzen has rightly commented:

> If the resurrection appearances are foundational events for the Christian Church, and if Jesus first appeared to a woman, then this would be a tremendous indictment on a church that for 2,000 years has suppressed the equal dignity of women and men, and has since its beginning refused to grant the proper recognition to the ministry of women in the structures of the church.[24]

Yet the story of Mary Magdalene is here in the gospels for us to recover, and the witness of her spiritual journey still calls us to the same faith. Even more, Jesus told the disciples on the evening of that same tremendous day: 'As the Father has sent me, so I send you' (John 20:21). He breathed the Holy Spirit on them and the story of the Church began. By her witness, Mary had played her part. Jesus still calls us, women and men, together to play our own parts in the great mission of God. Mary has led the way.

Questions for discussion

1. Why do you think the various myths and legends about Mary Magdalene arose? What can we learn from this?

2. Look at the gospel texts that refer to Mary Magdalene and construct your own summary of what we are able to learn from her story.

3. Imagine being one of the women who travelled with Jesus and the twelve, and share your thoughts on what that must have been like.

4. Try to construct a summary of how Mary Magdalene and the other women must have felt as they stood near the cross.

5. What do you think was the role of the angels in John's story? Compare this with angels in the other gospel accounts (Matthew 28, Mark 16, Luke 24). What are we to learn from this about the role of angels in the Bible?

6. Reflect on the meaning of Jesus' words to Mary in John 20:17.

7. Discuss the quotation from Thorwald Lorenzen towards the end of the study.

8. In what ways do you think that the story of Mary Magdalene constitutes a 'paradigm of discipleship'?

1. J Schaberg, *The Resurrection of Mary Magdalene. Legends, Apocrypha, and the Christian Testament* (New York: Continuum, 2002), p. 8.
2. See, for example, Schaberg, *The Resurrection of Mary Magdalene*, pp. 121–203; E de Boer, *Mary Magdalene. Beyond the Myth* (Harrisburg: Trinity Press, 1997), pp. 74–117.
3. Schaberg, *The Resurrection of Mary Magdalene*, p. 81.
4. S Haskins, *Mary Magdalen. Myth and Metaphor* (New York: Riverhead, 1993), pp. 96–97.
5. See M Miles, *Image as Insight. Visual Understanding in Western Christianity and Secular Culture* (Boston: Beacon Press, 1985), pp. 80–81. Several images are reproduced between these pages.
6. Schaberg, *The Resurrection of Mary Magdalene*, p. 107.
7. See the discussion in Schaberg, *The Resurrection of Mary Magdalene*, pp. 100–101.
8. Schaberg, *The Resurrection of Mary Magdalene*, p. 77.
9. De Boer, *Mary Magdalene*, p. 39.
10. De Boer, *Mary Magdalene*, p. 42.
11. D Sayers, as cited by F Moloney, *Woman. First Among the Faithful* (Blackburn, Vic: Dove, 1984), p. 25.
12. Clopas is not to be confused with Cleopas mentioned in Luke 24:18; this Clopas is otherwise unknown.
13. JAT Robinson, as cited by PS Minear, 'We don't know where ... John 20:2', *Interpretation* 30 (1976), 127.
14. *Southern Baptist*, 17 July 1901, 160.
15. Minear, 'We don't know where', 127.
16. W Temple, *Readings in St John's Gospel* (London: Macmillan, 1961), p. 361.
17. Schaberg, *The Resurrection of Mary Magdalene*, p. 328.
18. CH Dodd, as cited by L Newbigin, *The Light Has Come* (Grand Rapids: Eerdmans, 1982), p. 265.
19. ES Fiorenza, *In Memory of Her. A Feminist Theological reconstruction of Christian Origins* (London: SCM 1983), p. 333.
20. B Myers, *Christ the Stranger: The Theology of Rowan Williams* (London: T&T Clark, 2012), pp. 7–9, 29.
21. P Stiles, *Trumped by Grace* (Montrose, Vic: Poetica Christi, 2015), p. 47.
22. Schaberg, *The Resurrection of Mary Magdalene*, pp. 330–31.
23. B Witherington III, *John's Wisdom. A Commentary on the Fourth Gospel* (Louisville: Westminster John Knox Press, 1995), p. 334.
24. T Lorenzen, *Resurrection and Discipleship. Interpretive Models, Biblical Reflections, Theological Consequences* (Maryknoll, New York: Orbis, 1995), p. 141.

'La Pêche miraculeuse', Picou, Henri Pierre, 19th century

CHAPTER TWELVE

WHAT IS GOING TO HAPPEN TO HIM? JESUS AND THE DISCIPLE WHOM HE LOVED
(JOHN 21:1–25)

All parents know—at least in theory—that they should not have any favourites among their children. When a mother shows by what she says and does that she has a favourite son, or a father shows favouritism to one daughter, there is commonly another child who is hurt—maybe even psychologically scarred for life, as some experts would claim. This is not the place to lecture on family dynamics but to remind us just how remarkable was the claim for one of Jesus' disciples that he was *the* one loved by Jesus. Of course Jesus loved them all. But this man—although a few have suggested it might have been a woman—is described as 'the one whom Jesus loved'. This is most probably why the author of the gospel—commonly believed to be this very disciple—never named the 'beloved disciple'.

135

Yet this gospel asserts that God loves the whole world and that he taught his followers to love one another. Later, the Apostle Peter endured some strange learning experiences before he was able quite emphatically to declare that 'God has no favourites' (Acts 10:34). We are told of Jesus that: 'having loved his own who were in the world, he loved them to the end' (13:1). How was it, then, that Jesus clearly loved this person in a special way and that all his fellows in that intimate group of twelve knew this? Have we stumbled into the theological minefield of God's special choice, of the doctrine of election? Or is it, rather, a simple affirmation that Jesus in his full humanity needed the love of one special friend who supported him and on whose loyalty he could count? Is that so remarkable? Surely the affirmation that we too—just like Jesus—need such spiritual and trustworthy friends is an encouragement for us to discover such friends.

However, one question needs to be asked. Is 'the beloved disciple' simply a literary device, a kind of 'type' for a believer? Controversial but influential scholar Rudolph Bultmann, for example, argued that the disciple was a representative figure intended to symbolise Gentile Christianity—although relatively few have followed him in this understanding.[1] Of course, he could be a historical person and also acquire a symbolic role. I am convinced—along with the majority of modern interpreters—that he was a 'concrete' person and that by studying what we are told about him we can understand more about the creation of this gospel.

The list of possible candidates in this detective-type investigation is remarkable but surely the more important challenge is what we are pursuing—how encountering Jesus can transform our lives.

Before pursuing the complex question of the identity of this disciple, it is necessary to look closely at the specific references to him and build up our understanding of his character and the role he plays in what we have by custom called the Gospel according to John.

LEARNING ABOUT 'THE BELOVED DISCIPLE'

There are only a few specific occasions when the narrative introduces the mysterious figure of 'the beloved disciple' as such (13:21–26; 19:25–27; 20:2–10; 21:1–26).

AT THE LAST SUPPER: JOHN 13:23–26

This is the scene at the farewell supper after Jesus has washed the disciples' feet. At the table Jesus announced that one of them would betray him. John says that the disciples looked at each other, although he does not add, as do the other gospels, that they each asked: 'Is it I, Lord?' (Mark 14:19 // Matthew 26:22 // Luke 22:23). In John's gospel, Peter motioned to 'the one whom Jesus loved' to ask Jesus who was meant. Jesus identified Judas but in such a way that the others did not know what was happening. This narrative is framed within the emphasis on Jesus' absolute love for his disciples and his command that they should love in a similar way (13:1, 34–35).

The other significant feature here is the way in which this disciple is depicted: 'reclining next to Jesus' (13:23). This of course was the customary form of dining at this time, when guests would be placed on a series of couches arranged in a U shape around the table. The guests would recline with their heads towards the table and their feet stretched out away from it. They leaned on their left elbows, which meant that the right hand was free to take the food. The place of honour was to the left of, and thus slightly behind, the principal person. The second place was to his right and the guest there could lay his head on the chest of the host. This was where the disciple was seated.[2] As Conway summarises: 'His appearance in this story does not occur initially through naming, nor through dialogue with Jesus, but instead through a description of his position in relation to Jesus'.[3]

But there is more. The wording is precisely the same as that used to describe the Son being 'in the bosom of the Father' (1:18). Just as Jesus was able to make God known, so the beloved disciple is uniquely able to make Jesus known. Beasley-

Murray concluded: 'behind this gospel is the testimony of one who was "close to the heart" of Jesus'.[4]

What cannot be missed is the sense of intimacy between Jesus and the disciple. As Raymond Brown puts it: 'The Disciple is as intimate with Jesus as Jesus is with the Father'.[5] This is, of course, what Jesus emphasised in his farewell discourse when he stressed the analogous and reciprocal nature of the love between the Father, himself and the disciples (14:21; 15:9). Yet only in the story of the family at Bethany and here does the gospel specify Jesus' love for individuals (John 11:3–5). Indeed, individual disciples who misunderstand him are named (see 14:5, 8–10) but the only male figures in the gospel presented in such closeness to Jesus are this disciple and Lazarus (11:3, 36). (This is precisely why some think that the disciple was Lazarus.)

Scholars have wondered why this significant figure is not introduced into the narrative until this late point. He does present a distinct antithesis to Judas: 'the good and bad extremes are brought into the spectrum of discipleship'.[6]

In all these ways the disciple is presented as both a unique individual and as the 'complete disciple' (as William Temple expressed it).[7] All disciples—then and now—are loved by the Father and the Son who will 'come and make their home with them' (14:21–23). We too are offered the special love of Jesus, not in any sense that excludes others, but we can marvel with the grateful intensity of the Apostle Paul that 'he loved me and gave himself for me' (Galatians 2: 20).

BENEATH THE CROSS (JOHN 19: 25–27)

As we have noticed in our studies of both Mary and Mary Magdalene, this disciple was the only male present on that hill of suffering. The main interest in the story is, of course, the words that Jesus spoke to his mother and to the disciple, neither of whom is given a personal name here. Jesus seems to mark the end of his earthly family associations and to inaugurate the new family of his followers.

So what may we learn from the disciple's presence before the cross? It shows that, along with the women who were there, he was loyal to Jesus and did not want him to suffer and die alone. He will later insist that what he has written is true (21:24), and so his eyewitness account of these last events in the earthly life of Jesus, so crucial to his theology, may be trusted. In particular, when the sacred body was pierced by a Roman spear, it is John who records that blood and water came from the body.[8] That this is an eyewitness report is emphasised: 'He who saw this has testified so that you also may believe. His testimony is true, and he knows that he tells the truth' (19:35). This suggests that the disciple had not taken Mary away to his home before the end, as was perhaps implied in the report: 'that he took her away from that hour into his own home' (19:27).

However, the main emphasis here is that both the decision not to break his bones—as was customary—and to spear his side are interpreted as fulfilment of scripture (19:36–37). The texts for 'the bones' are most probably Exodus 12:46 or Numbers 9:12, which both refer to the Passover, or even Psalm 34:20. The other scripture about the piercing of the body is Zechariah 12:10. The way in which the early church identified fulfilments of texts from the Hebrew Bible is not always clear to a modern reader but is consistent with contemporary modes of interpretation.

From these verses, we may find again an example of one whose belief in the purposes of God was unwavering, even when all seemed lost. Searching the Scriptures offered meaning and hope. This is, once again, a challenge to our own discipleship and our commitment to a belief that the written word (what we call the Bible) reveals the living Word of God and can guide us in life's darkest experiences.

AFTER THE RESURRECTION—AT THE TOMB (JOHN 20:1–10)

When Mary Magdalene discovered that the tomb was empty, it is surely significant that the first thing she did was to run and tell Simon Peter and 'the other disciple, the one whom Jesus loved' (20:2). The two men were again together, running to the tomb, and the beloved disciple arrived first but only peered in and did not enter. Peter rushed in and the other disciple later followed. John claims that when he saw the discarded clothes there this disciple 'believed' (20:8). FF Bruce suggests that the disciple saw what Peter had seen: 'but with the eye of faith he saw more. Like a flash it came home to him what had happened: the Lord had risen from the dead and left the tomb'.[9] In other words, he was the first to believe in the risen Jesus and did not require a special appearance to believe this. The majority of interpreters affirm this position.

However, the text is somewhat ambiguous. It does not actually declare just what the disciple believed, which is unusual. Why would the gospel then note that the disciples 'as yet did not understand the scripture (singular) that he must rise from the dead' (20:9)? Which scripture was meant is not explained. Some think it was Psalm 16:10. We are reminded of Luke's story of how some dejected disciples were taught by Jesus about 'the things about himself in all the scriptures' (Luke 24:27). Possibly it simply means that the disciple believed that the tomb was empty. However, most interpreters accept that the disciple really did believe in the resurrection at this point. William Temple contrasts Peter's understanding with the disciple's:

> Perhaps he who was in heart nearest to the Lord had some instinct of understanding which enabled him to interpret what he saw and grasp the truth; anyhow, the 'disciple whom Jesus loved' was the first to believe in His resurrection.[10]

Again, the judgement of Westcott in his classic commentary can help us understand the process involved:

> The use of the word ['believed'] used absolutely rather points to the calm patient acceptance of a mystery as yet in part inexplicable with full confidence in the divine love. The threefold sign of the stone removed, the empty sepulchre, the grave-clothes leisurely arranged, indicated something still to be more fully shown, and the apostle waited in trustful expectation for the interpretation.[11]

We may then see in the beloved disciple a model of faith, even if his belief needed to move in stages as more and more was made clear to him. That is still exactly how it is for most disciples!

AFTER THE RESURRECTION—AT THE LAKE (JOHN 21:1–24)

Most scholars agree that this chapter is something of an addition to the gospel, since the end of Chapter 20 sounds like a suitable end to the book. However, the chapter does provide a link between the resurrection of Jesus and the ongoing work of his church in the world which continues through the disciples who are specially commissioned by Jesus. A kind of epilogue to the gospel, the chapter offers a balance to the prologue at the beginning (1:1–18).

This is one of the most loved stories from the gospel. The story of the seven disciples gathered 'together' (21:2) is fascinating. Whenever they are together disciples are always open to fresh revelations of the Lord. That these disciples headed off to fish after all the tumult of the previous days is natural and understandable. The appearance of Jesus and the shared breakfast is an intimate memory for the writer. The miraculous catch is frequently cited as evidence of the blessing that follows obedience to the command of the Lord.

Peter is undoubtedly the central figure, as his threefold assertion of love in response to his Lord's repeated questioning and the Lord's triple commissioning restores him to leadership.[12]

However, the beloved disciple is also involved. He is the first to recognise Jesus, telling Peter: 'It is the Lord!' (21:7). He is thus both a witness and a mediator, helping Peter to experience his restoration. Then he plays no further part in the story until Peter asks Jesus what will happen to him. Jesus has just told Peter to follow him and the writer clearly alludes to this when the disciple is also described as 'following' the two friends.

By his question, Peter, now comforted and emboldened by his restoration, accentuates the comparison between the two followers. Told by Jesus that he will eventually be taken where he would not choose to be taken—a prophecy of his martyrdom—Peter rather boldly asks about his fellow-disciple: 'What about him?' Peter still has much to learn about being a true pastor, to tend all the sheep!

The rather sharp response by Jesus delineates the roles that the two will play: 'If it is my will that he remain until I come, what is that to you? Follow me!' (21:22). Here is an unambiguous report of Jesus promising to come again. As the gospel opened with 'in the beginning', echoing Genesis and the creation, so this story will encompass the whole of history until the consummation: 'until he comes' (1 Cor. 11:26).

Possibly Jesus was not referring so much to the disciple remaining alive but 'remaining' in a figurative sense through the continuing power of his words in the gospel. Both Peter and this disciple will have different yet equally significant roles in the life of the church. As CK Barrett writes: 'Peter is the head of the evangelistic and pastoral work of the church, but the beloved disciple is the guarantor of its tradition concerning Jesus. Both functions are necessary to the life of the church'.[13]

Indeed, there are several parallels with the ministry of the Paraclete or the Holy Spirit—as Jesus had promised—and the work of the writer of the gospel. Both are to *remain* with the disciples (14:17), *teach* them everything (14:26), *remind* the disciples of all that Jesus had said (14:26), *declare* what they have heard (16:13) and *glorify* Jesus (16:14). Beasley-Murray observes that this work of the Holy Spirit is exactly what the beloved disciple has done.[14]

As the text clarifies (21:23), the saying of Jesus had been taken to mean that Jesus had prophesied that the disciple would still be alive when Jesus returned to earth—but that was not what Jesus had said!

Why on earth is all this in the gospel? Surely it is because—as 21:24 claims—this is a kind of signature of the disciple who wrote the gospel and whose witness is undoubtedly true. Perhaps another hand from his community added the observation: '*We* (the Johannine community) know that his testimony is true'. There was much more that could be written, more than any library could hope to contain. This provides a kind of imprimatur of the church—'like a miniature letter of recommendation'[15]—as the authenticity and authority of the text is affirmed. As Newbigin puts it: 'The witness of the beloved disciple comes not as a disembodied word, but as the witness of a community which has found and still finds in that word the power of everlasting life' (see 20:31 and 1 John 1:1).[16]

These two verses offer us a glimpse into the life of the church that had been so intimately connected to this disciple. It seems probable that at the time this concluding section of the gospel was written the disciple had died. This had evidently caused considerable anxiety and disappointment. His community needed to understand precisely what Jesus had said. Perhaps some had begun to question the witness of the disciple and—as Jesus had not yet returned as many had expected—some advice and reassurance was needed.

THEN WHO WAS THE BELOVED DISCIPLE?

In short, no one really knows! The author's successful determination to conceal the identity of the beloved disciple means that no infallible answer can be given. Not that that has stopped innumerable commentators from arguing for one person or another.

A recent comprehensive academic discussion on this subject by James Charlesworth extended to 480 pages![17] In his survey he listed at least fifteen proposals, apart from the opinions of those who believed he was simply an ideal, a fictitious or symbolical figure. The possible candidates included Matthias, Apollos, Paul, the rich young ruler (we are told that Jesus loved him in Mark 10:21), Andrew (Simon Peter's brother), Nathaniel, Judas (the brother of Jesus), and Lazarus. Charlesworth's own original idea was that the disciple was Thomas.

The traditional view of course is that the author was the Apostle John—certainly the unanimous tradition in the early church was that the gospel was by a 'John'. There are some difficulties with this view, although a majority still hold to it. We noticed in John 21 that seven disciples were in the fishing group: Simon Peter, Thomas, Nathaniel, 'the sons of Zebedee' and two others. Clearly, therefore, one of those in the boat was the beloved disciple. But who? The sons of Zebedee were James and John (Mark 1:19) but John is never named in this gospel. Would someone write about himself as 'the beloved disciple'? It is a strange mixture of humility—being anonymous—and privilege: *the* beloved disciple.

Again, 'another disciple' was known to the high priest and so was able to gain admission for Peter and himself to enter the courtyard of the high priest where Jesus had been taken prisoner (18:15–16). That a Galilean such as John could have enjoyed this status is unlikely, though of course it is not claimed here that it was the disciple 'whom Jesus loved'.

Whatever the problems—and they are real—the best probability is that the Apostle John was the beloved disciple. Of course, we also recognise that the community of which John was such a founding and prominent figure played an active role in shaping and preserving the ideas and the stories that are in the gospel, but we may with confidence believe that we have an authoritative witness to Jesus Christ as the Son of God.

So once again we are confronted by the challenge and invitation of this priceless 'spiritual gospel'. No matter who wrote it, the purpose is unambiguous: 'These are written so that you may come to believe that Jesus is the Messiah, the Son of God, and that through believing you may have life in his name' (20:31).

This continues to happen. Malcolm Muggeridge became a Christian late in life and this is his witness:

> I too became aware that there really had been a man, Jesus, who was also God. I was conscious of his presence. He really had spoken those sublime words—I heard them. He really had died on a cross and risen from the dead. Otherwise how was it possible for me to meet him, as I did?[18]

The stories of how in the days of Jesus many whom he encountered began a spiritual journey that transformed their existence—in John's language they found in Jesus the Way, the Truth and the Life—remain as positive witnesses to us all these centuries later. As we travel on the journey to a deeper faith we may still find inspiration and guidance in the story which 'John' has written for us. We all may become disciples whom Jesus loves.

Questions for discussion

1. Are there special problems in naming one person as 'the disciple whom Jesus loved'? Would this have created problems among the twelve disciples? What does this say about the humanity of Jesus?

2. Should a Christian leader have 'special friends' within his/her congregation?

3. What does the depiction of the last supper in John suggest about relationships among the disciples?

4. Explore what Jesus meant when he told John: 'Here is your mother'.

5. Was this disciple the first to believe in the resurrection?

6. What do you think Jesus meant when he said that the disciple would 'remain until I come'?

7. Discuss the way in which so many have been proposed as the beloved disciple. Why was this term used in the gospel? Who do you think he was?

8. What would you say to someone who asked how we could possibly know that the stories about Jesus in the gospel were really true?

Further along the way

1. See the discussion in CM Conway, *Men and Women in the Fourth Gospel: Gender and Johannine Characterization* (Atlanta: Society of Biblical Literature, 1999), p. 178.

2. L Morris, *The Gospel According to John* (Grand Rapids: Eerdmans, 1977), p. 625.

3. Conway, *Men and Women in the Fourth Gospel*, p. 180.

4. G Beasley-Murray, *John* (Waco: Word, 1987), p. 238.

5. R Brown, *The Gospel According to John* (Vol 2, New York: Doubleday, 1970), p. 577.

6. Brown, *The Gospel According to John*, p. 577.

7. W Temple, *Readings in St John's Gospel* (London: Macmillan, 1961 [1939-40]), p. 210.

8. For a detailed discussion on the medical explanation of the water and blood and on the symbolism in John, see the discussion in Beasley-Murray, *John*, pp. 355–58. Some scholars trace a sacramental allusion here, with water representing baptism and blood signifying the eucharist.

9. FF Bruce, *The Gospel of John* (Basingstoke: Pickering & Inglis, 1983), p. 385.

10. Temple, *Readings in St John's Gospel*, p. 360.

11. BF Westcott, *The Gospel According to St. John* (London: John Murray, 1919), p. 290.

12. For a discussion of this chapter see my *On the Way to Faith*, pp. 95–103.

13. CK Barrett, as quoted by Bruner, *The Gospel of John*, p. 1250.

14. Beasley-Murray, *John*, pp. 417–18.

15. CS Keener, *The Gospel of John. A Commentary* (vol 2; Grand Rapids: Baker, 2003), p. 1240.

16. L Newbigin, *The Light Has Come* (Grand Rapids: Eerdmans, 1982), p. 281.

17. JH Charlesworth, *The Beloved Disciple. Whose Witness Validates the Gospel of John?* (Valley Forge, Penns.: Trinity Press, 1995).

18. M Muggeridge, *Jesus Rediscovered* (London: Fontana, 1969), p. 8.

CONCLUSION

Did you notice how John's gospel ended? If all the many things that Jesus did were written down: 'I suppose that the world could not contain the books that would be written' (21:25). The numerous libraries of the world today do contain millions of books that derive from 'what Jesus did'. They 'contain' them now only because of new electronic ways of keeping books!

How could I have the temerity to add to that huge catalogue of titles? Not because of any claims to originality or literary ambition, but because each generation needs to embrace the challenge of 'what Jesus did'. This is a deeply personal question and my hope and prayer is that these straightforward studies will stimulate readers to their own faith encounters with the Jesus whom I gladly confess as 'my Lord and my God'.

These studies have not been intended to advance any novel ideas but rather to urge each one of us to face the central issues that each encounter has suggested. I know that many points of interpretation might be disputed but I hope that the inescapable claims of Jesus Christ have been shown to be true and life-giving. I believe that these claims invite a serious and honest response.

We are wisely urged to begin at the beginning. Christianity rests solely on the person of Jesus Christ. That is why John opened his gospel with the most astonishing claims about Jesus—that he was the eternal Son of God who was sent from the Father to live as a human in the world that he created. Light, truth and love are defined and found uniquely in this One. The gospel ends with the stories of the resurrection and the confession of the disciples that Jesus is 'Lord and God'. So there is the foundation question—do I believe that Jesus is the Son of God?

We read how John the Baptist sounded a warning to the ancient promised people of God, urging them to return to their God and prepare for the new thing he was doing in their midst. When he saw Jesus, he declared: 'Behold the lamb of God that takes away the sin of the world'. At once we are confronted with the basic reality of the sin that is so destructive and alienating in our own lives and in the world. So, another question resounds across the ages: will I confess my sin? Do I believe that God sent his son in order to remove my sin and the sin of the world? To put it another way, do I believe that Jesus died on the cross for my sins?

Jesus was more than just a good man and a brilliant teacher, a miracle-worker and transformer of people. This most admired and wise teacher did not shrink from declaring that he was truly the Son of God. We are not free to affirm the truth of his teaching and at the same time ignore this most basic claim about who he was. This type of smorgasbord belief—selecting only what we find palatable—dishonours the integrity of the teacher.

Jesus was also prophetic in his condemnation of all that corrupts genuine religion, as we saw when he chased the moneychangers out of the temple. Being a disciple of Jesus means that there will be times when we too are incensed—when Christian witness is harmed by grubby hypocrites who harm innocent children—or wherever there is exploitation of the disadvantaged and needy.

Some difficult issues arose in our reflection on Jesus' controversy with 'the Jews'. Another genuine problem for people today as they consider the claims of Jesus is that we live in a time of religious pluralism. That is, many different religious traditions all compete side by side. This is probably the most pressing theological question of our time in a multicultural place like Australia, in an age of globalisation and when religious controversy is at the heart of major world problems.

It is fashionable to condemn Christianity, or any other religion which alone claims to have the truth. Ever since the Enlightenment we have been taught a relativism which insists that all religions are simply referring to the same reality but they just use different names for it. Like the six blind men who fingered an elephant and called it— depending on the part of the anatomy they had touched—a snake, a sword, a fan, a pillar, and a rope. The question is the same—only the answers differ.

Of course, we must maintain absolutely the freedom of religion. But does toleration mean that all religions are ultimately the same? John's gospel undoubtedly claims that Jesus is 'the way, the truth and the life' (14:6). Most evangelical Christians would maintain unequivocally that Jesus is the only saviour of humankind. As Lesslie Newbigin has suggested: 'As a human race we are on a journey and we need to know the road. It is not true that all roads lead to the top of the mountain. There are roads which lead over the precipice. In Christ we have been shown the road'.[1]

As Christians we should relate to other faiths with respect. We must witness to our deepest convictions. An open or blank mind is not asked for; rather we are witnessing to our heart beliefs. We are there to tell the story of Jesus. It is not our business to convert others—we may pray and work for that to happen, but it is only and always the Holy Spirit who can lead others to trust in Jesus. We should not confuse thoughtful and caring dialogue with a responsibility to witness to our Lord. But true dialogue—listening and learning as we share—will help us to be honest evangelists.

At the heart of this question is this belief—as in the gospel's inspired language: 'all who received him, who believed in his name, he gave power to become children of God' (1:12). If we truly believe in Jesus then we may claim this promise and receive a new identity among this family of God. As Henri

Further along the way

Nouwen writes: 'Spiritual identity means we are not what we do or what people say about us. And we are not what we have. We are the beloved daughters and sons of God'.

Each study posed a question for us. We may not feel we know enough and that we do not know where to begin. But nothing could be simpler than to start where we are. We are not expected to pass an intricate examination on doctrine. When Jesus says—as he did to so many in this gospel—'Follow me', he simply requests our sincerity and willingness to follow as much as we understand. That is a good beginning!

If we do follow him we must be prepared for the cost. As Kierkegaard once observed: 'It is so hard to believe because it is so hard to obey'. Jesus demands our total loyalty. The story of Judas reminded us that when we follow our own selfish ambitions and plans we too could end up betraying Jesus and his work in the world.

Following him will naturally evoke a joyous witness to what he has done in our lives. David Bosch described genuine Christian witness:

> We know only in part, but we do know. And we believe that the faith we profess is both true and just, and should be proclaimed. We do this, however, not as judges or lawyers, but as witnesses; not as soldiers but as envoys of peace; not as high-pressure sales-persons, but as ambassadors of the Servant Lord.[2]

We remember how Jesus insisted that just as the Father had sent him, so he would send his disciples (20:21). One dimension of our witness is to serve as Jesus served. Chapter after chapter we have seen something of how all this works out. We saw how women's lives were changed by their encounter with Jesus. His own mother was shown to be a model disciple, and Mary Magdalene became an 'apostle to the apostles'. A distraught father gratefully received back the life of a sick son. After a lifetime of pain and humiliation a disabled man was healed. Story after story speaks to us of the matchless promise of a new life and hope: 'For God so loved the world that he gave his only son so that everyone who believes in him may not perish but have eternal life' (3:16).

Conclusion

What should be our response? Belief demands commitment. If in imagination we stand where the two Marys and the beloved disciple stood, there on Golgotha, beneath the cross of Jesus, we will know just how committed Jesus was to his 'hour'. God committed himself—he gave his son—and we dare not quibble about our commitment!

In the quietness of your own heart may I encourage you to make this commitment, to affirm your belief in Jesus as Son of God and Lord of all? Share your commitment to him with others who can walk with you. Please come and travel further along the way to faith.

---

1 L Newbigin, *The Gospel in a Pluralist Society* (Grand Rapids: Eerdmans, 1989), p. 183. See also the helpful discussion in M Heim, *Is Christ the Only Way?* (Valley Forge: Judson, 1985).

2 D Bosch, *Transforming Mission. Paradigm Shifts in Theology of Mission* (Maryknoll, NY: Orbis, 1991), p. 489.

READING GUIDE

The following commentaries on John have been found most useful.

W Barclay, *The Gospel of John* (Daily Study Bible, 2 vols; Edinburgh: Saint Andrew Press, 1955).

CK Barrett, *The Gospel According to St. John* (2nd edn, London: SPCK, 1978).

GR Beasley-Murray, *John* (Word Biblical Commentary 36; Waco: Word Books, 1987).

RE Brown, *The Gospel According to John* (2 vols, Anchor Bible 29, 29a; New York: Doubleday, 1966–70).

FF Bruce, *The Gospel of John* (Basingstoke: Pickering & Inglis, 1983).

FD Bruner, *The Gospel of John. A Commentary* (Grand Rapids: Eerdmans, 2012).

B Byrne, *Life Abounding. A Reading of John's Gospel* (Collegeville, MN: Liturgical Press, 2014).

DA Carson, *The Gospel According to John* (Grand Rapids: Eerdmans, 1991).

FB Craddock, *John* (Knox Preaching Guides; Atlanta: John Knox Press, 1982).

CS Keener, *The Gospel of John. A Commentary* (2 vols, Peabody, Mass: Hendrickson, 2003).

AJ Kelly and FJ Moloney, *Experiencing God in the Gospel of John* (Paulist Press: New York, 2003).

C Kruse, *John* (Tyndale NTC: Grand Rapids: Eerdmans, 2003).

D Lee, *Flesh and Glory: Symbol, Gender and Theology in the Gospel of John* (New York: Crossroad, 2002).

JF McHugh (ed. GN Stanton), *John 1–4: A Critical and Exegetical Commentary* (International Critical Commentary; London: T & T Clark, 2009).

B Milne, *The Message of John: Here is Your King!* (Downers Grove, Ill: InterVarsity Press, 1993).

FJ Moloney, *The Gospel of John* (Sacra Pagina, 4; Collegeville, Minn: Liturgical Press, 1998).

L Morris, *The Gospel According to John* (New International Commentary; Grand Rapids: Eerdmans, 1995).

L Newbigin, *The Light Has Come: An Exposition of the Fourth Gospel* (Grand Rapids: Eerdmans, 1982).

W Temple, *Readings in St John's Gospel* (London: Macmillan, 1961[1939–40]).

BF Westcott, *The Gospel According to Saint John* (London: John Murray, 1908).

B Witherington III, *John's Wisdom. A Commentary on the Fourth Gospel* (Louisville, KY: Westminster John Knox Press, 1995).

Printed by Libri Plureos GmbH in Hamburg, Germany